Bible Nurture and Reader Series

From a child thou hast known
The HOLY SCRIPTURES
which are able to make
thee wise unto salvation.

Bible Nurture and Reader Series

Phonics
Teacher's Manual

Grade 2

Rod and Staff Publishers, Inc.
P.O. Box 3, Hwy. 172
Crockett, Kentucky 41413
Telephone: (606) 522-4348

BIBLE NURTURE AND READER SERIES

"If you train your children carefully until they are seven years old, they are already three-quarters educated." This quote recognizes the importance of the critical early years in molding a child's life. The influences of childhood become powerful, lasting impressions.

The type of schoolbooks used certainly affects the developing appetites of our children for reading material. We will not instill in them appreciation for godly values by feeding them frivolous nonsense. We hold the Bible to be the highest guide for life and the best source of training for our children. The Bible reveals God and His will. Proverbs 9:10 says, "The fear of the LORD is the beginning of wisdom: and the knowledge of the holy is understanding." It is important that our children are exposed to truth from the beginning of their learning experience.

For the student to be exposed to the truth of God's Word only in textbooks is not sufficient to give him the very best. It is necessary for the tutor, be he parent or other teacher, to be firmly rooted in the Word of God and have the power of God's presence in his life. The Bible must be treasured as God's message to mankind. On that conviction this series is built, with the Scriptures as its very substance.

This book is designed as part of a series and will be most effective if so use. The grade two material includes the following books.

Pupil's Reader Units 1–3	Phonics Workbook Unit 1
Pupil's Reader Units 4, 5	Phonics Workbook Units 2, 3
Reading Workbook Unit 1	Phonics Workbook Units 4, 5
Reading Workbook Unit 2	Reading Teacher's Manual
Reading Workbook Unit 3	Phonics Teacher's Manual
Reading Workbook Unit 4	
Reading Workbook Unit 5	

Copyright, 1987
By
Rod and Staff Publishers, Inc.
Crockett, Kentucky 41413

Printed in U.S.A

ISBN 978-07399-0383-4

Catalog no. 11292.3

13   14   15   —   17   16   15   14   13

Table of Contents

A Word of Appreciation

It is with thanksgiving to God that we present these textbooks to those who are concerned about the spiritual welfare of their children. We believe that children are a heritage of the Lord and a sacred trust and that we dare not fail them in any area of their lives.

The *Bible Nurture and Reader Series* is possible only because of the work and leading of God in the lives of many faithful servants of His. We think first of all of our parents, ministers, and teachers who had a concern for us and faithfully taught and nurtured us in the Word of God. We appreciate those who have had a vision of the need for textbooks based on the Bible and have given their encouragement and help in the writing and publishing of these books.

We appreciate the work of the author, Sister Lela Birky, who has a deep burden for Bible-based school texts to nurture children in the fear of God.

We want to give recognition to the fact that we have used ideas from many textbooks, workbooks, reference books, and other sources. Sister Amy Herr was the writer for the present revision of the workbooks and teacher's manuals. Acknowledgment is also given to Sisters Marla Martin and Pauline Witmer and many other teachers who have developed and shared helps for teaching this series. Much effort was again devoted to artwork for the new books.

The Lord has provided strength in weakness, grace in trials, wisdom because we have none, joy in service, victory in opposition, financial help, and faithful laborers in this work. May His Name receive honor and praise, and may we rejoice that we can be laborers together with Him.

Phonetic Symbols

/a/	as in *hat*	/ā/	as in *pay*
/e/	as in *yes*	/ē/	as in *see*
/i/	as in *sit*	/ī/	as in *by*
/o/	as in *top*	/ō/	as in *go*
/u/	as in *bug*	/ū/	as in *cube*
		/ōo/	as in *food*
/ä/	as in *swap*		
	same as /o/	/är/	as in *park*
/ô/	as in *saw*	/ėr/	as in *her, fir, bur,*
/oo/	as in *foot*		*earn,* and *worm*
		/ôr/	as in *corn*
/ou/	as in *out*		allowing /ōr/)
/oi/	as in *boy*	/ār/	as in *square* and *chair*
			(allowing /er/ or /ar/)
		/ēr/	as in *dear* and *deer*
/sh/	as in *she*		(allowing /ir/)
/ch/	as in *chop*	/ə/	the indefinite vowel sound
/wh/	as in *when*		heard in an unaccented syl-
/th/	as in *thin*		lable, representing any of
/th/	as in *that*		the five vowels as in a*lone,*
/ng/	as in *sing*		*listen, flexible, consider,*
/zh/	as in *measure*		*suppose.*

Until the schwa symbol is learned, unaccented syllables are given with short vowel sounds rather than the schwa. The apostrophe is used to represent the indefinite vowel sound in *le* syllables. Example: table (ta•b'l)

Unit 1

UNIT 1
General Plan

Unit one is a very basic review of the phonics studied in grade one. The lessons may be used to teach phonics to those children who have not had it in first grade, in which case you will need to supplement with much drill and practice.

Directions are given for teaching the lessons as new material. As you find your class readjusting to school and resuming the knowledge and skills they have not used over summer, you may find it workable to spend much less time and explanation on each lesson. You may also combine several sections of the lesson into one class session. Most lessons include exercises that review material taught in previous lessons.

As much as possible, check the children's workbooks in class, having them say their answers and discussing wrong responses to help them understand their errors. Let the children correct their mistakes with colored pencil or pen to distinguish between corrections and original answers. This class discussion may suffice for much of your evaluation of the children's progress. Occasional lessons are marked in the answer key as suitable ones for objective records to supplement your mental evaluation.

The extra activities suggested with some lessons may or may not be phonics related. Some will be more of a comprehension activity.

There is some correlation between the phonics and reading lessons, although not as much as in grade one. Aim to keep a matched pace through the units of the two workbooks.

Remove and file the unit test from the back of each workbook before you give them to the children.

Phonics Lessons   Unit 1

Lesson   **Page**

LESSON 1
Sounds: a, b, r, t

A. Letter Sounds—*workbook, page 6 (top)*

For each letter given between slash marks in these lesson plans, say the sound of the letter rather than the letter name.

Have the children open their phonics workbooks to Lesson 1. "What is the picture in the box at the beginning of the first row? What sound do you hear at the beginning of *apple*? What letter do you see under the apple? The letter *a* makes the /a/ sound. [Have the children practice forming the /a/ sound.] Listen as I say the names of the pictures in that row."

Row 1: ant, sun, ax, alligator, apron

"Did you hear any words that begin with /a/?" Let the children name those pictures and underline them with their pencils. Then tell them to put their pencils in their desks as you do the rest of the page orally. When you later assign the page for individual work, the first row may serve as a sample to remind the children how to do the exercise.

"What is the first picture in the second row? What sound do you hear at the beginning of *box*? What letter do you see under the box?" Practice the /b/ sound orally, then let the children say the names of the pictures in the row and analyze the first sound of each one.

Row 2: glasses, bib, egg, pin, ball

"What will you do in this row when I tell you to use your pencils? The directions are at the top of the page. Look at them while I read them."

Proceed in a similar way for the next two rows of pictures.

Row 3—rug: bread, rabbit, rooster, rain, feather
Row 4—tent: turtle, dog, toes, pencil, top

Assign the exercise as seatwork.

B. Using the Sounds—*workbook, page 6 (bottom)*

Have the children go to the board and print the letters they have studied on the phonics page as you dictate the sounds. (Pay attention to correct formation of letters.) Then pronounce words beginning with those four sounds and have the children print the letters for the sound at the beginning of each word. You may name the pictures in the exercise at the bottom of page 6 or compile your own list of words.

After board practice have the children look at the directions for the bottom of page 6. Give any help needed for them to understand the directions and assign the written exercise.

C. Letter Forms—*workbook, page 7*

Print on the board the capital and small forms of the letters studied or refer to them on alphabet cards posted on the wall. Drill the children on the letter sounds by pointing to the various letters (either form) and having them respond with the sound of the letter. You may again dictate letter sounds and have the children print the capital form for each one.

Direct attention to page 7 of the phonics workbook and explain the directions. Assign the page as written work.

D. Sounding Words—*workbook, page 7 (edge)*

Tell the children that *a* is a vowel and the other letters you have studied are consonants. We sound consonants and vowels together to make words. Print on the board the two-letter combinations that are found in the list at the edge of page 7. Help the children to sound the combinations; then add consonants after the vowels to make words.

Let the children silently practice the list on the edge of page 7 and then read it aloud.

ANSWER KEY

Page 6 (top) *All pictures are named. The words in bold print indicate underlined pictures.*

apple: **ant**, sun, **ax**, **alligator**, apron

box: glasses, **bib**, egg, pin, **ball**

rug: bread, **rabbit**, **rooster**, **rain**, feather

tent: **turtle**, dog, **toes**, pencil, **top**

Page 6 (bottom) *The whole word is printed for each picture for certain identification. The letter in bold print indicates the child's response.*

t able, *b* ell, *b* at, *a* nimals, *t* en

r ose, *t* ape, *r* attle,
a mbulance, *b* arn

Page 7 (top)

Page 7 (middle)

a	b	r
t	a	b
r	t	a

(bottom)

T	B	A
A	R	B
R	T	R

EXTRA ACTIVITY

In the space below the edge list on page 7, have the children draw a bat and print the word to label it.

LESSON 2
Sounds: e, s, d, g

A. Letter Sounds—*workbook, page 8 (top)*

Have the children put their pencils away and do the exercise as an oral activity. "What is the picture at the beginning of the first row? What sound do you hear at the beginning of *egg*? That is the sound of the letter *e* that you see below the egg. What is the next picture in the row? With what sound does *bird* begin? What is the next picture? What do you hear at the beginning of *elephant*? Is that the sound you hear at the beginning of *egg*?

How will you mark the elephant? What is the next picture? . . . "

Assign the exercise as written work.

B. Using the Sounds—*workbook, page 8 (bottom)*

Dictate the sounds of the new letters for the children to print on the board. Also review the letters studied in Lesson 1. Watch for any confusion of *b* and *d*. A helpful guide may be to point out the likeness of the lower case *b* to the capital with the top curve missing.

Pronounce words for the children to print the initial sound.

Assign the part as seatwork.

C. Letter Forms—*workbook, page 9 (top three parts)*

Teach the associated forms by printing them on the board or referring to wall cards that show both the capital and small letters. Review the sounds of the letters by having the children print capitals for the sounds you say. Also dictate combinations for the children to print if they are capable of doing so.

Explain the directions for the three exercises before assigning them as seatwork.

D. Sounding Words—*workbook, page 9 (bottom)*

Tell the children that *e* is a vowel and let them name the letter from Lesson 1 that is also a vowel. Print on the board two-letter combinations from the edge list and help the children to sound them. Add final consonants and sound the words.

Have the children practice the combinations and words in the edge list and read them aloud.

Do the bottom part on page 9 as a class exercise. Let someone sound the two combinations with the first picture. Then ask what the picture shows and see if they recognize the combination used at the beginning of the word. Tell them to circle the correct letters.

ANSWER KEY

Page 8 (top)

egg: bird, *elephant*, *engine*, olive, tree

sun: *saw*, vase, *star*, kettle, *scissors*

dog: *door*, *duck*, cat, *doll*, *doughnut*

girl: *gate*, hand, *glasses*, *gum*, salt

Page 8 (bottom)

s oap, *b* one, *s* andwich, *t* wo, *d* ish

r oof, *e* nvelope, *d* esk, *g* un, *a* nt

Page 9 (top)

Page 9

(second part)				(third part)			
a	b	g	s	E	G	D	S
e	r	d	t	A	R	B	T

Page 9 (bottom)

se ven, *de* sk, *ga* s

ta ck, *re* d, *ba* g

EXTRA ACTIVITY

Tell the children to go back over

Lessons 1 and 2 and color all the pictures of animals. If you have allowed them to color the pictures as they did each lesson, tell them to circle all the animal pictures.

LESSON 3
Sounds: i, f, n, p

A. Letter Sounds—*workbook, page 10 (top)*

"What is the picture at the beginning of the first row? What sound do you hear at the beginning of *Indian*? That is the sound of the letter *i* that you see below the Indian. What is the next picture in the row? With what sound does it begin? What is the next picture? What do you hear at the beginning of *wing*? Is that the sound you hear at the beginning of *Indian*? What is the next picture? What do you hear at the beginning of *ink*? Is that the sound in *Indian*? How will you mark the picture? What is the next picture? . . ."

Assign the exercise as written work.

B. Using the Sounds—*workbook, page 10 (bottom)*

Dictate the sounds of the new letters for the children to print on the board. Include review of previously studied letters. Then pronounce words for them to print the initial sounds.

Assign the workbook exercises.

C. Letter Forms—*workbook, page 11 (top three parts)*

Teach the associated forms and assign the exercises on page 11.

D. Sounding Words—*workbook, page 11 (bottom and edge)*

Let the children name the vowels they have studied and see if they can tell you which letter studied in Lesson 3 is a vowel. Print combinations and words on the board and give the children practice in joining these words; then have them study the edge list silently before reading it aloud.

Do a few of the examples on the bottom of page 11 with the class; then let them finish on their own.

ANSWER KEY

Page 10 (top)

Indian: ice cream, wing, ***ink***,
   comb, ***igloo***

four: ***flower***, cup, ***fork***, ***fire***,
   ladder

nail: chair, ***nut***, mouse, ***nose***,
   leaf

pin: moon, ***pie***, ***pear***, water,
   pig

Page 10 (bottom)
d ipper, *p* umpkin, *f* an, *g* oat,
   a pple
b ear, *n* est, *E* skimo, *i* gloo,
   r ope

Page 11 (top)

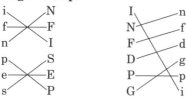

Page 11
(second part)   (third part)

n	f	e	g	F	N	P	I
p	i	d	s	E	S	D	G

Page 11 (bottom)
fi nger, *pa* n, *ne* st, *bi* b
si x, *pe* n, *fe* nce, *di* sh

LESSON 4
Sounds: o, h, c, k

A. Letter Sounds—*workbook, page 12 (top)*
Follow the procedure as in previous lessons. Tell the children that we have two letters that make the /k/ sound.

B. Using the Sounds—*workbook, page 12 (bottom)*
If you teach the children that *c* makes the /k/ sound before /a/ and /o/, and *k* makes the /k/ sound before /e/ and /i/, they will be able to use the correct letters for the pictures with initial /k/ sounds. Print *ca, ke, ki,* and *co* in a column on the board reference.

Otherwise you may tell the class to use *c* for any word that begins with /k/ in the first row and *k* for any word that begins with /k/ in the second row.

C. Letter Forms—*workbook, page 13 (top three parts)*
Follow the procedure as in previous lessons.

D. Sounding Words—*workbook, page 13 (bottom and edge)*
Help the children to combine the new sounds in combinations and words. Have them study the edge list silently and then read it aloud and do the exercise at the bottom of page 13.

ANSWER KEY

Page 12 (top)
ox: tire, block, man, *olive,*
   octopus
hat: rake, *hammer*, *hoe*,
   hand, watch

cup: letter, jug, *comb*, *cane*,
   car
king: *key*, spoon, *kite*, meal,
   fox

Page 12 (bottom)
h ive, *f* ive, *c* alf, *t* ent,
   I ndian
n ewspaper, *k* ettle, *h* ook,
   p otato, *o* strich

Page 13 (top)

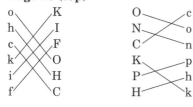

Page 13
(second part)	(third part)
o k i p	O C F K
c h f n	I H N P

Page 13 (bottom)
co b, *ca* ndy, *fo* x, *hi* ll
so cks, *he* n, *bo* ttle, *ki* ng

EXTRA ACTIVITY
   Have the children look back over the pictures for Lessons 1–4 and put an *x* on every picture that shows something to eat.

LESSON 5
Sound of /u/ and Rules for *c* and *k*

A. Letter Sounds—*workbook, page 14 (top and middle)*
Review the vowel sounds you have studied and introduce the new one. Drill the five vowel sounds in order until the children can rattle them off without concentration—/a, e, i, o, u/. They should then be able to rapidly read the columns of combinations on page 14.

B. Using the Sounds—*workbook, page 14 (bottom)*
Have the children try each of the vowels in the blank for the first word in the exercise. They should recognize that they can make a number of words, but only one word is correct for the picture. Tell them to print the letter of the correct sound in the blank.
You may want to have individuals read the lists of combinations to you while the class is working on this assignment.

C. Letter Forms—*workbook, page 15 (top)*
Teach the capital form of *u* and assign this review exercise.

D. Sounding Words—*workbook, page 15 (edge)*
Have the children practice the edge list silently and then read the words aloud.

E. The Rules for *c* and *k*—*workbook, page 15 (middle and bottom)*
Teach the children that when /k/ is heard at the beginning of a word, we use *c* if the next letter in the word is *a*, *o*, or *u*. We use *k* if the next letter is *e* or *i*. When /k/ comes at the end of a short vowel word, we use the *c* and *k* together. Print some sample words on the board for the children to apply the rules before they begin the exercise in the workbook.

ANSWER KEY

Page 14 (top)

under: leaf, *up*, mitten, *umbrella*, fish

Page 14 (bottom)

1. b *a* t
2. h *e* n
3. h *o* p
4. r *u* g
5. n *e* t
6. p *i* g
7. f *a* n
8. k *i* ss

9. b *u* s
10. b *u* d
11. b *u* g
12. c *a* p
13. h *o* t
14. c *o* b
15. t *e* n
16. f *i* n

Page 15 (top)

b	c	d	f	g
h	k	n	p	r
s	t	i	o	u

Page 15 (bottom)

1. *c* an
2. *k* it
3. ta *ck*
4. *c* ub
5. du *ck*
6. *c* ot
7. ne *ck*
8. *k* in
9. *k* eg
10. *c* ut
11. ro *ck*
12. *c* ob
13. *k* en
14. si *ck*
15. *c* at

EXTRA ACTIVITY

Let the children take the words from the bottom part on page 14 and make as many words as they can, substituting different vowels. Have them print the words on a paper beside numbers corresponding to the numbers in the workbook.

LESSON 6
Sounds: ā, m, w, l

A. Letter Sounds—*workbook, page 16, (top)*

"What is the first picture in the first row? What sound do you hear at the beginning of *acorn*? What letter do you see under the acorn? The letter *a* can have the /a/ sound or the /ā/ sound. See the macron above the *a*. Whenever you have a macron over the an *a*, you know it says /ā/ and not /a/. What is the next picture in the row? . . . "

B. Using the Sounds—*workbook, page 16 (bottom)*

Tell the children to place a macron over the *a* if they find any pictures beginning with the /ā/ sound.

C. Letter Forms—*workbook, page 17 (top)*

Self-explanatory.

D. Sounding Words—*workbook, page 17 (middle and edge)*

Self-explanatory.

E. The Silent *e* Rule—*workbook, page 17 (bottom)*

"Sometimes *a* says /a/ in a word and sometimes *a* says /ā/. [Print the word *mad* on the board and let someone sound it. Add an *e*.] The *e* on the end does not make any sound. But when the *e* is there, *a* says /ā/." Use *cap* for another sample. Assign the last part of the lesson. Have the children read both words for each number after they have done the exercise.

ANSWER KEY

Page 16 (top)

acorn: **apron**, cheese, **aitch**, apple, cake

mouse: broom, **man**, **moon**, nose, **mop**

wing: grapes, vase, **well**, **window**, **web**

lamb: **ladder**, pig, rose, **lamp**, yoke

Page 16 (bottom)

w atch, *h* ouse, eight (*ā*), *l* etter, *m* oney

l eaf, *w* agon, *m* atch, *p* umpkin, *s* aw

Page 17 (top)

l — M
w — L
m — W
k — H
h — C
c — K

M——m
P — l
L — n
N — w
W — p
F——f

Page 17 (middle)

ma p, *we* b, *le* g, *mu* d
wi g, *lo* ck, *mo* p, *li* ps

Page 17 (bottom)

1. pane   5. dame
2. rate   6. cane
3. mane   7. hate
4. fade   8. gape

Gradebook: There are 60 points for the entire lesson, counting every picture in the first exercise and allowing 2 points for good oral reading of the edge list.

LESSON 7
Sounds: ē, v, y, z

A. Letter Sounds—*workbook, page 18 (top)*
Proceed as for Lesson 6.

B. Using the Sounds—*workbook, page 18 (bottom)*
Review the rule that /k/ before *a, o,* or *u* is spelled with *c,* or accept *k* for the beginning sound of *cup.*

C. Letter Forms—*workbook, page 19 (top)*
Self-explanatory.

D. Sounding Words—*workbook, page 19 (middle and edge)*
Proceed as for previous lessons.

E. The Digraph *ee*—workbook, page 19 (bottom)*
Teach the children to pronounce the /ē/ sound for words which have two *e*'s together. Have them circle the /ē/ words and read the words aloud.

ANSWER KEY

Page 18 (top)
eagle: egg, *eat*, *eel*, pear,
   turtle
violet: ball, nine, *vase*, top,
   vine
yarn: heart, *yoke*, jacket,
   yak, *yard*
zoo: *zipper*, *zebra*, pocket,
   zero, fan

Page 18 (bottom)
b us, *w* ing, *z* ig-zag, *y* am,
   l id
m ailbox, *v* est, *y* o-yo, *c* up,
   v egetables

Page 19 (top)

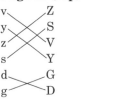

Page 19 (middle)
va n, *ve* st, *ya* k, *zi* pper

Page 19 (bottom)

1. reed	9.
2.	10. beet
3. seen	11. deed
4. peep	12.
5.	13. seed
6. teen	14. need
7. meet	15.
8.	16.

17. peel	25. feet
18.	26. peek
19.	27. seek
20. feel	28. reef
21. keen	29
22.	30.
23.	31. heel
24. keel	32.

LESSON 8
Sounds: ī, j, qu, x

A. Letter Sounds—*workbook, page 20 (top)*
   Teach the sound of *qu* as a blend of the two consonant sounds /k/ and /w/. Tell the children that we always print a *u* after q in words.
   Teach the sound of *x* as a blend of the two consonant sounds /k/ and /s/. Tell them to listen for that sound at the end of words because we do not begin words with /ks/.

B. Using the Sounds—*workbook, page 20 (bottom)*
   Review again the rule for using *c* before *a*, *o*, or *u* and *k* before *e* or *i*. Tell the children to use a macron if they find any words that begin with /ī/.

C. Letter Forms—*workbook, page 21 (top)*
   Self-explanatory.

D. Sounding Words—*workbook, page 21 (second part and edge)*
   Point out again that the /ks/ sound is found at the end of words.

E. The Silent *e* Rule—*workbook, page 21 (last two parts)*

Review the silent *e* rule and apply it to sample words with the letter *i* on the board.

ANSWER KEY

Page 20 (top)

ice: dime, Indian, *icicle*, pin, *idol*

jam: *jacks*, chair, hand, *jacket*, *jar*

quilt: *question mark*, cane, *quail*, shoe, *queen*

ax: duck, hammer, *box*, clock, *fox*

Page 20 (bottom)

qu iver, *c* ake, *y* arn, *j* et, *z* ebra

j unk, *k* ing, *ī* vy, *w* indow, *v* ase

Page 21 (top)

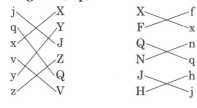

Page 21 (second part)

ju g, *qua* ck, *ox*, s *ix*

Page 21 (third part)

1. hide   5. pine
2. dime   6. dine
3. wine   7. ripe
4. quite   8 kite

Page 21 (bottom)

1. Jane   4. dive
2.   5. daze
3. keep   6.
          7. quake   10.
          8.   11. weed
          9. vine   12. heel

EXTRA ACTIVITY

Have the children look over the pictures in Lessons 5–8 and circle all the pictures that show something to wear.

LESSON 9
Sound of /ō/

A. Letter Sounds—*workbook, page 22*

Introduce the /ō/ sound and symbol.

Tell the children that they have learned all the letters in the alphabet. That is why there are no new consonants in this lesson. Drill all the consonant sounds in a thorough review with flash cards or by pointing to the letters on wall cards.

B. Letter Forms—*workbook, page 23 (top)*

Say the alphabet with the children and point out that this exercise has all the letters in the usual order which is called alphabetical order.

C. The Silent *e* Rule—*workbook, page 23 (bottom)*

Practice the long vowel rule and apply it to *o* words such as *hop, ton, not, cod, mop,* and *rod.* Have the children read the words as an oral exercise.

ANSWER KEY

Page 22 (top)

oak: *ocean*, octopus, *oval*, *old*, flower

Page 22 (bottom)

h and, *p* otato, *l* ion, *c* up, *n* ose

t ail, *b* ed, *y* ard, *m* itten, *qu* estion mark

k ite, *w* ell, *j* ar, *d* oor, *z* ipper

f ish, *v* est, *r* ainbow, *g* arden, *s* un

Page 23 (top)

a b c d e
f g h i j k
l m n o p
q r s t u
v w x y z

Page 23 (bottom)

1.	8. deep
2. home	9. wife
3. gaze	10.
4. five	11.
5.	12. jeep
6.	13. yoke
7. cave	14.

15. vote	22. quite
16. cake	23.
17.	24. joke
18. kite	25. beef
19.	26.
20.	27. fame
21. need	28.

Gradebook: 79 points for the whole lesson

LESSON 10
Sound of /ū/

A. Letter Sounds—*workbook, page 24*

Introduce the /ū/ sound and symbol.

Print the five vowels on the board and let the children point to the one that tells which vowel sound they hear as you pronounce words. Put a macron over each vowel and say words with long vowel sounds for them to again show which sound they hear.

Make sure the children understand the directions for the second part of page 24 and assign the exercise.

B. Letter Forms—*workbook, page 25 (top)*

Review the alphabet again. Have the children print all the capital letters.

C. Long Vowel Rules—*workbook, page 25 (bottom)*

Review the silent *e* rule and the digraph *ee*.

Teach the children how to make a neat macron that covers exactly one letter. Make sure they understand that it is to be over the vowel that shows the vowel sound they hear. In the words with double *e* the macron should be over the first *e*.

ANSWER KEY

Page 24 (top)

universe: mule, yarn,
    umbrella, ***uniform***, heart

Page 24 (bottom)

b *u* g	h *a* t	n *u* t	c *o* b
w *e* b	l *i* d	b *e* d	t *o* p
c *ā* ne	r *ō* se	b *ē* e	f *ī* ve
t *ū* be	r *ā* in	s *ō* ap	m *ū* sic
f *ē* et	k *ī* te	b *ā* le	k *ē* y
b *ō* ne	m *ū* le	p *ī* e	l *ē* af

Page 25 (top)

A B C D E
F G H I J K
L M N O P
Q R S T U
V W X Y Z

Page 25 (bottom)

1. dīve	8.
2. cūte	9. mēek
3.	10.
4. wēep	11. wāde
5.	12. mūte
6. bōne	13
7. gāte	14. cōve

15. jāde	22. fēel
16.	23.
17. tīme	24. nōte
18.	25. mūle
19. quēen	26. līke
20. hāze	27.
21. cūbe	28. vōte

EXTRA ACTIVITY

Let the children try printing the whole word for some pictures at the bottom of page 24.

LESSON 11
Spellings of /ā/ and Final Consonants

A. Spellings of /ā/—*workbook, page 26*

The children have studied the /ā/ sound in relation to final silent *e*. Help them to recognize *a-e* as a form of that rule. The hyphen represents any consonant that may be heard at the end of the word. Introduce *ai* and *ay* as other spellings of the /ā/ sound. Teach the rule that *ai* is used within a word and *ay* is used at the end of a word. Tell the children that *y* is a vowel when it is used this way.

The columns at the top of the page are to be finished by printing in each word the letters at the head of the column. Ask the children which letters should be used in the first word on the bottom part of the page and have them tell the reason why. Discuss a few more samples and have the children finish the page, printing the correct long *a* spelling in each word.

B. Final Consonant Sounds—*workbook, page 27 (top)*

Tell the children to put their pencils away and do the exercise orally as a class activity. Have the children say the names of the pictures and identify the sound they hear at the end of each word.

Assign the exercise as written work.

C. Long Vowel Rules—*workbook, page 27 (bottom)*

Teach the children to put a macron over only the *a* in the /ā/ digraphs.

ANSWER KEY

Page 26

g a t *e*	w *ai* t	d *ay*
s a v *e*	t *ai* l	l *ay*
b a l *e*	p *ai* n	r *ay*

1. h *ay*
2. h *ai* l
3. h *a* t *e*
4. s *ay*
5. w *ay*
6. G *ai* l
7. J *a* n *e*
8. m *a* k *e*
9. m *ay*
10. m *ai* d
11. n *a* m *e*
12. v *ai* n
13. F *ay*
14. J *a* k *e*

15. r *ai* d	22. p *ay*
16. g *ay*	23. c *a* m *e*
17. w *a* k *e*	24. b *ai* t
18. f *a* d *e*	25. l *a* t *e*
19. J *ay*	26. l *ai* d
20. d *a* z *e*	27. K *ay*
21. f *ai* l	28. m *ai* n

Page 27 (top)

ea *r*, bi *b*, li *d*, ga *s*, boa *t*

hea *d*, hor *s* e, cri *b*, ha *t*,

  eigh *t*

ca *r*, fou *r*, bu *s*, roa *d*, tu *b*

Page 27 (bottom)

1. wēek	7. sāil
2. dāte	8. pūre
3.	9. wāy
4. pāid	10.
5.	11. hōpe
6. līne	12. gāve
13.	19. nōte
14. mīne	20. māil
15. fāme	21. cūte
16. pāy	22.
17.	23.
18. hēel	24. bāy

LESSON 12
Spellings of /ē/ and Final Consonants

A. Spellings of /ē/—*workbook, page 28*

Review the digraph *ee* and teach the digraph *ea*. Teach the children that when an *e* at the end of a word is the only vowel in the word, it also has the long sound.

The children are to complete the words in each column with the letters at the head of the column, and then choose words from the lists they have finished to print in the sentences at the bottom of the page.

B. Final Consonant Sounds—*workbook, page 29 (top)*

You may again want to use the exercise for oral practice before assigning it as written work. Have the children say the words to recognize the sound at the end of each one.

C. Long Vowel Rules—*workbook, page 29 (bottom)*
Review the final *e* rule and the /ā/ digraphs.
Print these words on the board and let the children show how they think
the long vowels should be marked.

deep	hem	me
rail	seat	tap
leg	we	meal

ANSWER KEY

Page 28 (top)

s *ee*	t *ea*	b *e*
f *ee*	p *ea*	h *e*
m *ee* k	h *ea* t	m *e*
w *ee* p	s *ea* m	w *e*
b *ee* f	r *ea* d	y *e*

Page 28 (bottom)
1. heat
2. weep
3. see
4. read
5. he, me

Page 29 (top)
pi *n*, nai *l*, pi *g*, cu *p*, shel *f*
whee *l*, roo *f*, su *n*, ru *g*, fa *n*
le *g*, tra *p*, cal *f*, tai *l*, ro *p* e

Page 29 (bottom)

1. fīne	7.
2. dāy	8. wē
3. Lēe	9. vōte
4.	10. fēet
5. zēal	11.
6.	12. bēan
13. wēed	19.
14.	20. bē
15.	21. rāin
16. tūne	22.
17. mē	23. sēa
18. pāle	24.

EXTRA ACTIVITY
Tell the children to draw pictures to illustrate some of the sentences at the bottom of page 28.

LESSON 13
Spellings of /ī/ and Final Consonants

A. Spellings of /ī/—*workbook, page 30*
Review *i-e* and teach the digraph *ie*. Tell the children that *y* is also a vowel when it comes at the end of a word and there is no other vowel in the word. The letter *y* has the /ī/ sound.
Have the children consider the first two words on the bottom of the page. "Which long *i* spelling should be used? How can you tell?" (The wider answer space indicates that the two-letter diagraph is to be used.)
Assign the page as written work.

B. Final Consonant Sounds—*workbook, page 31 (top)*
Proceed as for previous lessons.

C. Vowel Identification—*workbook, page 31 (bottom)*

Review *y* as a vowel in the digraph *ay* and when it is the only vowel in a word.

Teach the children to circle their letters carefully so they do not include any letters that are not supposed to be circled and go around the whole letter of those that should be.

ANSWER KEY

Page 30

b i t e	d *ie*	b *y*
l i m e	l *ie*	m *y*
p i p e	t *ie* d	fr *y*

1. sk *y*
2. p *ie*
3. n i n e
4. cr *y*
5. d i v e
6. t *ie*
7. p i l e

8. v *ie*
9. h i k e
10. b *y*
11. d *ie* d
12. d *ie*
13. s i d e
14. f *ie*

15. f i l e
16. l *ie*
17. f i v e
18. t *ie* d
19. tr *y*
20. l i f e
21. r i p e

22. t *ie*
23. w i d e
24. m *y*
25. d *ie*
26. l *ie* d
27. tr *ie* d
28. m i r e

Page 31 (top)

thu *m* b, si *x*, wa *v* e, fuz *z*, cage (*j*)

bo *x*, co *m* b, a *x*, broo *m*, sto *v* e

hedge (*j*), gu *m*, fi *v* e, rose (*z*), fo *x*

Page 31 (bottom)

1. ea	8. i e	15. y	22. a e
2. ay	9. i	16. u	23. i e
3. u	10. y	17. ay	24. y
4. ie	11. a	18. i	25. e
5. i	12. ee	19. ie	26. o e
6. y	13. ay	20. y	27. e
7. u e	14. ay	21. o	28. ai

Gradebook: 80 points for the entire lesson, counting each correct word as 1 point

LESSON 14
Spellings of /ō/

A. Spellings of /ō/—*workbook, page 32*

Review *o-e* and teach the digraphs *oa* and *ow*. Tell the children that *ow* is to be used at the end of words, and in this case, *w* is a vowel.

Have the children use the spellings at the top of the page to finish the words at the bottom.

B. More Spellings of /ō/—*workbook, page 33 (left side)*

Introduce two more long *o* spellings to be used at the end of words. Ask the children how they will know which spellings to use for the words at the bottom of the page.

The two pages should not be mixed as one exercise because the children would have no basis on which to decide whether to print *ow* or *oe* for the words with a wide blank at the end.

C. Long Vowel Rules—*workbook, page 33 (right side)*
Review the long vowel rules and digraphs you have studied.

ANSWER KEY

Page 32

c o n *e*	c *oa* l	b *ow*
h o m *e*	f *oa* m	m *ow*
p o k *e*	s *oa* p	s *ow*

1. t o n *e*	7. l *oa* f
2. t *oa* d	8. r *ow*
3. w o v *e*	9. c *oa* x
4. l *ow*	10. r o p *e*
5. r *oa* m	11. g *oa* t
6. s *ow*	12. m o l *e*

13. m *oa* n	19. c o d *e*
14. j o k *e*	20. t *ow*
15. b o n *e*	21. g *oa* l
16. b *oa* t	22. m *ow*
17. h o p *e*	23. c *oa* t
18. b *ow*	24. v o t *e*

Page 33 (left side)

d *oe*	g *o*
w *oe*	h *o*
J *oe*	n *o*

1. f *oe*	7. h *o*
2. l *o*	8. d *oe*
3. s *o*	9. n *o*
4. t *oe*	10. h *oe*
5. g *o*	11. r *oe*
6. w *oe*	12. s *o*

Page 33 (right side)

1. hīde		16. bōat
2. wōe		17. wē
3.		18. nō
4. cōke		19. fōe
5. gō		20.
6. tēa		21. wāit
7. hōle		22. hōax
8. tūbe		23. tīe
9.		24. lōw
10. lāy		25.
11. rōw		26. sō
12. lōan		27.
13. mēet		28. nōte
14.		29. cāke
15. dōe		30. bōw

EXTRA ACTIVITY

Circle the number of each action word in the list on the right side of page 33.

LESSON 15
Spellings of /ū/ and Double Consonant Endings

A. Spellings of /ū/—*workbook, page 34*

Review *u-e* and introduce *ew*. *W* is again a vowel in this digraph.

Have the children finish the words with the correct spelling, and then choose from the lists in the top part of the page to complete the sentences at the bottom.

B. Final Consonant Sounds—*workbook, page 35 (top)*

Tell the children that these sounds at the end of short vowel words are usually printed with two letters. Have them print two letters for the final sound of each picture.

C. Vowel Identification—*workbook, page 35 (bottom)*

Review the instances when *y* and *w* are vowels.

Encourage the children to be neat and exact in circling the letters.

ANSWER KEY

Page 34 (top)

c u b e   m u l e   n *ew*   m *ew*
c u t e   t u n e   f *ew*   d *ew*

Page 34 (middle)

m *ew*   d u n e   p *ew*   t u b e
c u r e   f u m e   y *ew*   f *ew*
h *ew*   m u t e   p u r e   n *ew*

Page 34 (bottom)

1. few
2. cube
3. new
4. mule

Page 35 (top)

clo *ck*,   we *ll*,   dre *ss*,   cu *ff*,
  be *ll*

du *ck*,   fu *zz*,   blo *ck*,   hi *ll*,
  cla *ss*

pi *ll*,   ta *ck*,   ki *ss*,   pu *ff*,   tru *ck*

Page 35 (bottom)

1. i e	6. ow	11. ew	16. y
2. ay	7. ai	12. ie	17. oe
3. oa	8. e	13. ay	18. ea
4. a e	9. u e	14. o	19. ow
5. ew	10. y	15. ee	20. o e

LESSON 16
Digraphs: sh, wh

A. Consonant Digraphs—*workbook, page 36 (top and middle)*

"What is the first picture in the top row? What sound do you hear at the beginning of *sheep*? What letters do you see under the sheep? When we have these two letters together, they stand for the /sh/ sound. What is the next picture in the row? What sound do you hear at the beginning of *thimble*? . . ."

Teach the children to differentiate between /w/ and /wh/. Tell them to blow while they make the /w/ sound to say /wh/. If they do not make this speech distinction in their vocabulary, have them listen as you say the words for the pictures.

Have the children print the digraph for the beginning sound of each picture in the middle of the page.

B. Sounding Words—*workbook, page 36 (bottom)*

Have the children sound the words in each section and draw lines to match the correct vowel sound to each word. The matching could be figured out by knowledge of the rules for long vowel spellings. Make sure the children do sound the words by having them read aloud.

C. Initial and Final Consonants—*workbook, page 37*

Review the use of *c* and *k* before certain vowels.

Review the ending sounds that are spelled with two consonants after short vowels. Have the children check the page for them after they have printed the sounds and see that two letters are printed where they belong.

ANSWER KEY

Page 36 (top)
sheep: thimble, spoon, fish,
 shoe, shell
whale: ***whip***, chair, ***wheel***,
 vase, wing

Page 36 (middle)
wh eat, ***sh*** ip, ***wh*** istle, ***sh*** irt,
 wh eelbarrow

Page 36 (bottom)

1. shop	a		11. sheet	ā
2. shuck	e		12. shade	ē
3. shack	i		13. show	ī
4. shed	o		14. shine	i
5. shin	u		15. ship	ō
6. when	ē		16. shell	ā
7. which	ī		17. sheep	e
8. what	o		18. shy	ē
9. wheat	e		19. shock	ī
10. while	i		20. shape	o

Page 37

v i n e, *l i d*, *d* re *ss*, *g u m*

w a v e, *qu* ee *n*, *f u zz*, *s i x*

n e *ck*, *b i b*, *z* ippe *r*, *j u g*

c u *ff*, *p i ll*, *h a t*, *t o p*

m a n, *y* ar *d*, *r o ck*, *k i t* e

Gradebook: 40 points for page 37

EXTRA ACTIVITY

Classify pictures on page 37 by putting an *x* on the things that people can make and putting a circle around the things that only God can make.

LESSON 17
Digraphs: ch, th, th̲

A. Consonant Digraphs—*workbook, page 38 (top and middle)*

Teach the difference between /th/ and /t̲h̲/. The sounds are formed in the same way by the mouth, but /th/ is only the sound of forced air and /t̲h̲/ carries a voiced sound with it.

B. Using the Sounds—*workbook, page 38 (bottom)*

Have the children print the digraph for the beginning sound of each picture.

C. Double Consonant Rule—*workbook, page 39*

Have the children read the words at the top of the page and then copy them in the correct place according to vowel sounds.

After they have sorted the words, they are to follow the directions at the bottom of the page and complete the sentence. Discuss the rule with the children to make sure they understand the lesson of the page.

ANSWER KEY

Page 38 (top)
cherries: ***chimney***, cat, shell, ***chin***, ***chair***
thorns: bag, ***thumb***, tree, ***thimble***, fire

Page 38 (middle)
they: ***this***, thin, thick, ***the***, ***then***

Page 38 (bottom)
th rone, *wh* istle, *sh* ovel, *ch* ain
wh eel, *ch* eckers, *wh* ale, *th* ermometer
th istle, *sh* epherd, *ch* urch, *sh* oe

Page 39 (middle)
long vowel words

daze	use
sail	deal
soak	leaf
rake	loaf
file	dike
haze	wife

short vowel words

pu *ff*	mi *ss*
ja *ck*	fi *zz*
le *ss*	pa *ss*
te *ll*	hu *ff*
bu *zz*	du *ll*
fi *ll*	do *ck*

Page 39 (bottom) *The bold print letters in the last two columns should be circled.*
Use *ck, ff, ll, ss,* and *zz* at the end of words with the ***short*** vowel sound.

LESSON 18
Final Digraphs and Medial Consonants

A. Ending Consonant Digraphs—*workbook, page 40 (top)*

Give some oral practice by saying the words for the pictures in the exercise or other words that end with consonant digraph sounds for the children to identify.

Assign the exercise as written work.

B. Medial Consonant Sounds—*workbook, page 40 (bottom)*

First help the children to recognize separately sounded syllables by getting them to repeat two-syllable words after you. It may help to use a beating motion of the hand or silently clap the hands for each syllable.

Then listen for the sound at the end of the first syllable, and print that sound in the blank. Make sure the children realize they are to limit their answers to the four consonants given with the directions.

C. Double Consonant Endings—*workbook, page 41 (top)*

Review the rule at the end of Lesson 17.

Review the rules for long vowels and let the children find some words in which they recognize long vowel spellings. Tell the children to put a macron over each long vowel in the list of words. Then have them go back over the words and print one letter for for the final sound of the long vowel words and two letters for the words in which they did not mark the vowel. The letters at the head of each column are to be used for all the words in that column.

D. Long Vowel Spellings—*workbook, page 41 (bottom)*

Help the children to understand that there is a column of spelling on each side of the center column of vowel sounds, and every spelling must have a line drawn to the middle column. Some answers will have more than one line drawn to them because there is more than one way to spell the long vowel sounds.

ANSWER KEY

Page 40 (top)

ben *ch*, mo *th*, fi *sh*, pea *ch*,
  ba *th*

mat *ch*, di *sh*, bran *ch*, tee *th*,
  bru *sh*

Page 40 (bottom)

bo *t* tle, sho *v* el, pe *n* ny,
  ru *l* er, bu *t* ter

po *n* y, se *v* en, bu *t* ton,
  pe *n* cil, tu *l* ip

Page 41 (top)

1. sha *ck*
2. du *ck*
3. s ō a *k*
4. j ō *k* e
5. chi *ck*
6. l ē a *k*
7. sho *ck*
8. f ē e *l*
9. wh ī *l* e
10. she *ll*
11. se *ll*
12. s ē a *l*
13. ye *ll*
14. qui *ll*

15. whi *ff*
16. b ē e *f*
17. cha *ff*
18. l ī *f* e
19. l ē a *f*
20. b u *ff*
21. sh ē a *f*

22. fu *ss*
23. ū s e
24. che *ss*

25. whi *zz*
26. g ā *z* e
27. d ō *z* e

Page 41 (bottom)

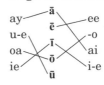

EXTRA ACTIVITY

The following is an oral exercise that can be conducted by an older student if the teacher does not have the extra time. Many of the questions have multiple answers. The more the children find, the better.

Turn to Lesson 18. Find a picture that—

  a. makes you think of eating. (dish, teeth, peach)
  b. makes you think of summertime. (moth, peach, tulip)

c. shows something that belongs in a desk. (ruler, pencil)

d. makes you think of the story of Zacchaeus. (tree branch, money)

Turn to Lesson 17. Find a picture that—

a. is something for a child to use. (checkers, whistle)

b. is something for a man to use. (shovel, chain)

c. is something for a woman to use. (thimble)

d. makes you think of the story of Jonah. (whale)

Turn to Lesson 16. Find a picture that—

a. would be in the kitchen. (spoon, chair, lid, jug)

b. would be in the ocean. (fish, whale, ship, wave, shell)

c. would be in a yard. (vine, dandelion fuzz, yard, rock)

d. would be in the sky. (wing, kite)

e. is something to wear. (shoe, shirt, dress, bib, zipper, hat, cuff)

LESSON 19
More Medial Consonants

A. Medial Consonant Sounds—*workbook, page 42*

Let the children say the words for the pictures for the sake of hearing the number of syllables. Then say the words again, listening for the consonant sound in the middle.

The page is presented in two sections to narrow the selection to fewer possibilities in each part.

B. Vowel Identification—*workbook, page 43 (top)*

Review the usage of *y* and *w* as vowels.

C. Digraph Definition—*workbook, page 43 (middle and bottom)*

Read the definition with the children and look at the list of digraphs. Let the children say the sound made by each digraph. Assign the bottom of the page as written work.

ANSWER KEY

Page 42 (top)

ra *b* bit, bu *z* zard, mu *f* fin,
  ru *b* bers, ca *r* rot
li *z* ard, ta *b* le, ru *f* fle,
  ca *b* bage, ba *r* rel

Page 42 (bottom)

di *p* per, whi *s* tle, pu *d* dle,
  ha *m* mer, pu *p* py
cra *d* le, bu *g* gy, a *p* ple,
  thi *s* tle, pa *p* er

Page 43 (top)

1. o	9. ay	17. u e	25. ie
2. e	10. a e	18. ea	26. i
3. e	11. ay	19. ow	27. y
4. ew	12. oe	20. a	28. ew
5. e	13. y	21. ee	29. e
6. ai	14. ee	22. ow	30. a
7. a	15. o	23. i e	31. y
8. o e	16. ea	24. u	32. oa

Page 43 (bottom)

vowel digraphs

ea	ew	ai
oe	ay	ie
ow	ee	oa

consonant digraphs

ch	th
wh	th
sh	ck

Gradebook: 52 points for page 42 and 43 (top)

LESSON 20
Medial Digraphs

A. Medial Consonant Digraphs—*workbook, page 44 (top)*

Explain that *ck* is a digraph as well as the other pairs of letters that form new sounds when they are put together. Listen for the digraph sounds in the middle of the words.

B. Digraph Definition—*workbook, page 44 (middle and bottom)*

Make sure the children understand the directions. See if they can tell you what the sentence will say before filling it in.

C. Rule for *c* and *k*—*workbook, page 45 (top)*

Review the rule that *c* is used before *a*, *o*, and *u*, and *k* is used before *i* and *e*. Have the children fill in the first row to use as reference when they do the lists of words.

D. Double Consonant Endings—*workbook, page 45 (bottom)*

Review the rule that some letters need to be doubled at the end of a short vowel word. Ask the children to tell you what those particular letters are. Include *ck*.

ANSWER KEY

Page 44 (top)

pit *ch* er, bu *ck* le, bu *sh* el,
bu *ck* et, fea *th* er
fi *sh* ing, po *ck* et, ben *ch* es,
mo *th* er, fa *th* er

Page 44 (middle)

ch	sh	ay (ā)	ea (ē)	oe (ō)
wh	th	ai (ā)	ie (ī)	ow (ō)
ck	th	ee (ē)	oa (ō)	ew (ū)

Page 44 (bottom)

A digraph is **two letters** together that make **one sound**.

Page 45 (top)

c a *k* e *k* i *c* o *c* u

1. *k* eep	5. *c* ap
2. *c* ute	6. *c* ube
3. *c* atch	7. *k* eg
4. *c* ob	8. *k* een
9. *k* in	13. *c* ave
10. *c* og	14. *c* oax
11. *c* ure	15. *k* it
12. *k* ite	16. *c* up

Page 45 (bottom)

1. dul *l*	6. buz *z*
2.	7. tic *k*
3. pas *s*	8.
4.	9.
5. muf *f*	10.

11.	16. wel *l*
12.	17.
13. mus *s*	18.
14. fiz *z*	19. lac *k*
15.	20.

EXTRA ACTIVITY

Turn back to the word lists on page 43 (top). Have the children underline all the consonant digraphs with red crayon and all the vowel digraphs with green.

LESSON 21
Blends With *s*

A. Consonant Blends—*workbook, page 46*

Introduce each blend by having the children sound the two letters close together. Have them practice some of the words in each list with both blends given, and tell which blend makes a correct word. Also notice that some words will be correct with either blend.

After the top of the page is done, the children are to choose words from the lists they completed to finish the sentences at the bottom. All sentence blanks need words which had only one correct choice above.

B. The Rule for *c* and *k*—*workbook, page 47 (top)*

The familiar rule of *c* before *a, o,* or *u*; and *k* before *e* or *i* still applies when the *c* or *k* is part of a blend. Point out the word in which *y* follows the blank. Tell the children to think of the vowel sound that *y* makes and to use the letter that belongs with that sound.

C. Long Vowels—*workbook, page 47 (middle)*

You may want to point out number 17. "What long vowel sound does the word have? [ū] Does the word have a *u* to mark with a macron? Have the children print the vowel symbol after the word.

D. Definitions—*workbook, page 47 (bottom)*

Read the definitions with the children and see if they can complete number 2 without looking back for the words.

ANSWER KEY

Page 46 (top)

st op	*sp* in
st ack	*st* uck
sp ell	*st* ill / *sp* ill

sn ake	*sl* ip
sm oke	*sl* ay / *sw* ay
sn eak	*sl* ow
sn eeze	*sl* eet / *sw* eet
sm ile	*sl* eep / *sw* eep
sn ow	*sl* op

Page 46 (bottom)
1. smile
2. smoke
3. slow
4. snake

11.
12. stāin
13.
14. tīe
15.

16. slōpe
17. stew (ū)
18. slāte
19. shōw
20.

Page 47 (top)
1. *sc* ab   4. *sk* id   7. *sk* etch
2. *sk* in   5. *sc* ale   8. *sc* off
3. *sc* ope   6. *sk* y   9. *sc* um

Page 47 (bottom)
2. A digraph is **two letters** together that make **one sound.**

Page 47 (middle)
1.
2. bōat
3.
4. stāy
5. tūne

6. sēat
7. slīde
8.
9. spēak
10.

LESSON 22
Blends: bl, br, cl, cr, fl, fr

A. Consonant Blends—*workbook, page 48*
Have the children practice orally, trying both blends in the blanks for some of the words.

The sentences below can all be finished by using words from the middle column above. You may let the children discover that for themselves or tell them if you think they need the help.

B. The Alphabet—*workbook, page 49 (top)*
Have the class practice saying the alphabet orally. Remind the children to print all lower case letters in the exercise.

C. Definitions—*workbook, page 49 (middle)*
Drill the definitions and call for recitation from a number of the children.

D. Digraphs—*workbook, page 49 (bottom)*
Caution the children not to include any blends with the digraphs.

ANSWER KEY

Page 48 (top)

br aid*	**bl** ush / **br** ush	**cl** ean	**fl** ock / **fr** ock
br oke	**bl** ame	**cr** eam	**fl** ash
bl ack	**bl** eed / **br** eed	**cl** uck	**fl** og / **fr** og
*Allow **blaid** unless you do this		**cl** ip	**fl** esh / **fr** esh
one as a sample with the class and		**cr** eek	**fl** y / **fr** y
tell them that blade *has the final* e		**cr** ib	**fr** oze
spelling.			

Page 48 (bottom)
1. crib
2. clean
3. cluck
4. cream
5. creek

Page 49 (top)
b, d, f, h, j
l, n, p, r, t,
   v, x, z

Page 49 (middle)
1. A blend is **two letters** that make **two sounds** close together.
2. A digraph is **two letters** together that make **one sound.**

Page 49 (bottom) *The letters in bold print should be circled, and the ones in brackets should be in boxes.*

1. sn *ow*
2. c *oa* [ch]
3. h *oe*
4. bl *ow*
5. [sh] o [ck]
6. cl *ay*
7. [th] *ee*
8. [wh] *ee* l

9. [ch] *ew*
10. f *ai* [th]
11. t *ie* d
12. st *ay*
13. [wh] *ea* t
14. bla [ck]
15. [ch] *ai* n
16. *oa* [th]

There are 14 vowel digraphs and 11 consonant digraphs.

EXTRA ACTIVITY
Have the children turn to the lists of words on pages 46 (top) and 48 (top) and mark all the long vowels with macrons. The *y* in *fly* or *fry* should not be marked with a macron, but the letter *i* may be printed after the word and marked.

LESSON 23
Blends: gl, gr, pl, pr, tr, tw

A. Blends—*workbook, page 50*
Proceed as for previous lessons. The sentences can all be finished with words from the third list.

B. The Alphabet—*workbook, page 51 (top)*
Self-explanatory.

C. Rules—*workbook, page 51 (middle and bottom)*
Review the definitions and have the children show that they understand them by following the directions for the bottom of the page. Have them do number 1 for the entire part, and then start over and do number 2, and lastly number 3.

ANSWER KEY

Page 50 (top)

gr een	*gr* ip	*pl* um	*tw* ig
gl ad	*gl* ow / *gr* ow	*pr* each	*tw* in
gr ape	*gl* aze / *gr* aze	*pr* ess	*tr* y
pl ay / *pr* ay	*tr* ack	*pr* ide	*tr* ain
		pl an	*tr* ade

Page 50 (bottom)
1. twin
2. track
3. try
4. twig
5. trade

Page 51 (top)
c, e, g, i
k, m, o, q, s
u, w, y

Page 51 (middle)
1. A *digraph* is two letters together that make one sound.
2. A *blend* is two letters that make two sounds close together.

Page 51 (bottom) *All bold print letters should be circled, the ones in brackets should be in boxes, and the blends should be underlined.*
1. pl *ay*
2. fr *ee* ze
3. [wh] ip
4. bl u [sh]
5. [ch] *ea* p
6. pr *ea* [ch]
7. cl a [sh]
8. sw i [sh]

9. [th] i [ck]
10. gr *ow*
11. st a [ck]
12. tr u [ck]
13. st *ew*
14. fl *oa* t
15. t *ee* [th]
16. [sh] *ee* p

There are 9 vowel digraphs, 12 consonant digraphs, and 11 blends.

Gradebook: 69 points for the entire lesson

LESSON 24
Triple Blends

A. Blends—*workbook, page 52*
Explain to the children that sometimes three consonants can be together and we hear all three sounds. This is also called a blend. Help them to sound the triple blends to finish the words.

Discuss the rewording of the definition at the bottom of the page.

You may specify the number of words you want the children to use in their sentences.

B. The Alphabet—*workbook, page 53 (top)*
Self-explanatory.

C. Review of Vowels and Consonants—*workbook, page 53 (middle)*
Have the children follow the directions for number 1 for the whole exercise, then do number 2, and last do number 3.

D. Pronunciation Symbols—*workbook, page 53 (bottom)*
Self-explanatory.

ANSWER KEY

Page 52 (top)

dr eam / *scr* eam	*scr* ub	*str* ap	*spr* ee
dr ess	*scr* ap	*str* ay / *spr* ay	*str* eam
dr ill	*dr* y	*str* ain / *spr* ain	*str* etch

Page 52 (middle) *Individual work.*

Page 52 (bottom)
A *blend* is two or more letters that sound close together.

Page 53 (top)
b c,   e f,   h i
k l,   n o,   q r
t u,   w x,   z

Page 53 (middle) *The long vowels should be marked with macrons, the blends should be underlined, and the consonant digraphs shown here in brackets should be in boxes.*

1. l ī e   6. d ō e
2. [wh] ē el   7. sp ō ke
3. [ch] ō ke   8. str ā y
4. cr ō w   9. sm a [sh]
5. gl ē e   10. c ū te

11. br u [sh]   16. [wh] ī te
12. ō a [th]   17. cr ā ne

13. [th] ī ne   18. scr at [ch]
14. spr ā in   19. s ō
15. [sh] ē   20. t ē a [ch]

There are 17 long vowels, 9 consonant blends, 10 consonant digraphs.

Page 53 (bottom)
1. a   6. b
2. d   7. c
3. e   8. a
4. b   9. e
5. c   10. d

EXTRA ACTIVITY
Have the children draw pictures for some of the original sentences they have printed on page 52.

LESSON 25
Three-Letter Blends

A. Blends—*workbook, page 54*
Shr and *thr* blend a digraph and consonant. Help the children to sound the new blends.

B. The Alphabet—*workbook, page 55 (top)*
Self-explanatory.

C. Digraphs and Blends—*workbook, page 55 (middle)*
Make sure the children pay careful attention to the directions again.

D. Pronunciation Symbols—*workbook, page 55 (bottom)*
Have the children pronounce the words by sounding the symbols and finding the words in the list above as an oral exercise before they do the written work.

ANSWER KEY

Page 54 (top)

squ eak	*spl* ash / *squ* ash	*thr* ow	*thr* ee
squ eeze	*squ* eal	*thr* one	*thr* oat
spl it	*spl* int / *squ* int	*shr* ug	*shr* ub

Page 54 (bottom)
1. throne
2. splash
3. Three
4. throw
5. squeeze
6. shrub

Page 55 (top)
a b,   d e f,   hi
j k,   m n o p q
  s t u v,   x y z

Page 55 (middle) *The letters in bold print should be circled, the digraphs in brackets should be in boxes, and the blends should be underlined.*

1. [th] is
2. str ike
3. [sh] *ee* p
4. [wh] y
5. f *ew*
6. [ch] *ai* n
7. spl a [sh]
8. sn *ow*

9. str u [ck]
10. [wh] ite
11. sl *ow*
12. str *ay*
13. sp *ea* k
14. c *oa* [ch]
15. spr y
16. sp e [ck]

There are 8 vowel digraphs, 9 consonant digraphs, 9 consonant blends.

Page 55 (bottom)
1. speak
2. few
3. strike
4. coach
5. why
6. this
7. chain
8. snow

LESSON 26
Review

A. Review of Terms—*workbook, page 56 (top)*
Self-explanatory.

B. Double Consonant Endings—*workbook, page 56 (bottom)*
Review the rule. Ask the children to find a word that should have a double consonant and does not. Ask them to find a word that has a double consonant but should not because there is a long vowel in the word.

C. The Alphabet—*workbook, page 57*
Give some oral drill for the children to practice supplying the letters that come before and after a given letter.

D. Rule for *c* and *k*—*workbook, page 57 (bottom)*
Review the use of *c* or *k* before each of the vowels, and teach the children to use *c* before any consonant.
Have them fill in the blank before each vowel, and then use that row and the rule as a guide for the rest of the exercise.

ANSWER KEY

Page 56 (top)
1. d
2. e
3. a
4. c
5. b
6. h
7. f
8. i
9. j
10. g

Page 56 (bottom)

1. elok   5. fluf
2. maill   6.
3.   7. swel
4. loaff   8.
   9. elas   13.   17. buz
   10. weeek   14.   18.
   11.   15.   19.
   12.   16.   20. bles

Page 57 (top)

a – c	i – k	q – s
v – x	o – q	m – o
g – i	c – e	s – u
x – z	k – m	e – g

Page 57 (bottom)

c a   *k* e   *k* i   *c* o   *c* u

1. *c* lip   7. tri *ck*   13. *c* rash
2. *k* ill   8. *c* oat   14. la *k* e
3. *c* row   9. ba *k* e   15. *k* eep
4. sha *ck*   10. see *k*   16. stru *ck*
5. di *k* e   11. *c* ub   17. jo *k* e
6. *c* ave   12. *c* lutch   18. pea *k*

Gradebook: 77 points for the entire lesson

EXTRA ACTIVITY
Print correctly on a paper each of the misspelled words found in the exercise on page 56 (bottom).

LESSON 27
Final Blends

A. Final Blends—*workbook, page 58*
Help the children to sound the final blends and have them read the lists orally.

B. The Alphabet—*workbook, page 59 (top)*
Self-explanatory.

C. Original Sentences—*workbook, page 59 (bottom)*
You may want to specify the number of words used or the number of sentences constructed.

ANSWER KEY

Page 58

ne *st*	be *lt*	de *sk*	cla *sp*
che *st*	fe *lt*	a *sk*	gra *sp*
la *st*	ti *lt*	du *sk*	wi *sp*
twi *st*	qui *lt*	bri *sk*	cri *sp*
cru *st*			
ze *st*			
fa *st*	she *lf*	ye *lp*	mi *lk*
mi *st*	gu *lf*	he *lp*	si *lk*
we *st*	se *lf*	gu *lp*	su *lk*

Page 59 (top)

l – n	d – f	n – p
h – j	w – y	f – h
b – d	p – r	t – v
r – t	v – x	j – l

Page 59 (bottom) *Individual work.*

LESSON 28
More Final Blends

A. Final Blends—*workbook, page 60*

Help the children to sound the final blends and have them read the lists orally.

B. The Final Blends *nd* and *nt*—workbook, page 61*

Make sure the children clearly sound the letters in these ending blends. Have them sound some words with both choices and tell which one is correct. Some words are correct with either ending.

After the lists of words are completed, the children are to use those words in the sentences below.

ANSWER KEY

Page 60

la *mp*	sku *nk*
pu *mp*	bu *nk*
ca *mp*	ba *nk*
sta *mp*	wi *nk*
bu *mp*	thi *nk*
da *mp*	ya *nk*
ju *mp*	bli *nk*
stu *mp*	ju *nk*
clu *mp*	cra *nk*
li *mp*	tru *nk*

fa *ct*	te *xt*
tra *ct*	ne *xt*
du *ct*	
	gi *ft*
we *pt*	le *ft*
ke *pt*	shi *ft*
scri *pt*	dra *ft*
sle *pt*	tu *ft*
cre *pt*	swi *ft*

Page 61 (top)

1. pa *nt*	5. ba *nd*
2. ha *nd*	6. sla *nt*
3. sa *nd*	7. sta *nd*
4. pai *nt*	8. po *nd*

9. spe *nd* / spe *nt*
10. we *nt* / we *nd*
11. la *nd*
12. hu *nt*
13. gru *nt*
14. be *nd* / be *nt*
15. se *nd* / se *nt*
16. gra *nd* / gra *nt*

Page 61 (bottom)

1. sand / pond	5. pond
2. hand	6. stand
3. hunt	7. pant
4. paint	

EXTRA ACTIVITY

Have the children draw pictures to illustrate some of the sentences at the bottom of page 61.

LESSON 29
Other Endings

A. Endings *ng* and *nch*—*workbook, page 62 (top and middle)*

Help the children to sound the endings *ng* and *nch*. The ending *ng* is a digraph and *nch* is a blend of the two consonant sounds /n/ and /ch/.

Do the first two parts of page 62 with the class as an oral exercise, and then assign them as written work.

B. Special Endings with /ī/—*workbook, page 62 (bottom)*

Tell the children that the vowel *i* sometimes has the long sound when it is not a part of a digraph and the word does not end in *e*. The vowel *i* usually has the long sound before the final blends *ld* and *nd*.

C. The Alphabet—*workbook, page 63 (top)*

Self-explanatory.

D. Special Endings With /ō/—*workbook, page 63 (middle)*

Tell the children that the vowel *o* has the long sound when followed by these pairs of consonants.

E. Long Vowels—*workbook, page 63 (bottom)*

Have the children repeat the spellings which produce the long *i* and *o* and apply the rule in marking the vowels.

ANSWER KEY

Page 62 (top)

1. ba **ng**	4. swi **ng**
2. si **ng**	5. be **nch**
3. lu **ng** / lu **nch**	6. thi **ng**

7. spri **ng**
8. pi **ng** / pi **nch**
9. cru **nch**
10. fi **nch**
11. ra **ng** / ra **nch**
12. stri **ng**

Page 26 (middle)

1. A **blend** is two or more letters that sound close together.
2. A **digraph** is two letters together that make one sound.
3. ng

Page 62 (bottom) *Letters in bold print should be circled.*

1. k ī **nd**	5. m ī **nd**
2.	6.
3. ch ī **ld**	7. m ī **ld**
4.	8. w ī **nd**
9.	13.
10.	14. gr ī **nd**
11. f ī **nd**	15.
12. w ī **ld**	16.

Page 63 (top)

j – l	t – v	e – g
p – r	a – c	o – q
f – h	r – t	w – y
u – w	k – m	b – d

Page 63 (middle) *Letters in bold print should be circled.*

1. p ō *st*
2. c ō *ld*
3.
4. t ō *ll*
5.

6.
7. str ō *ll*
8. b ō *lt*
9. m ō *st*
10.

11. h ō *st*
12.
13. sc ō *ld*
14.
15. c ō *lt*

16. g ō *ld*
17. j ō *lt*
18.
19. h ō *ld*
20. r ō *ll*

Page 63 (bottom)

1. fl ē et
2. bl ī nd
3. sh ī ne
7. t ī e
8. m ō lt
9. t ē ach

4. sn ō w
5. f ā ith
6. scr ō ll
10. str ā y
11. c ō ax
12. f ō ld

LESSON 30
Review

A. Phonics Terms—*workbook, page 64 (top)*
The questions may well be used for oral review before the page is assigned.

B. Endings With Long *i* and *o*—*workbook, page 64 (middle)*
Review again the consonant endings that follow /ī/ and /ō/.

C. Vowel Identification—*workbook, page 64 (bottom)*
Self-explanatory.

D. Long Vowels, Digraphs, and Blends—*workbook, page 65*
IMPORTANT—Have the children do the page four times over, following a different step of the directions each time and counting their answers to check each step.

ANSWER KEY

Page 64 (top) *Individual work.*

Page 64 (middle)

1. s ō ld
2.
3. m ī ld

4.
5. k ī nd
6. c ō lt

7. f ī nd
8. p ō st
9.

10.
11. w ī ld
12. r ō ll

Page 64 (bottom)

1. tr *y*
2. fl *ow*
5. w *e*
6. b *y*

3. st *ay*
4. y *e* ll
7. h *ew*
8. w *ai* l

Page 65 *The long vowels are marked with macrons, the consonant digraphs are underlined, the* *initial consonant blends in bold print should be circled, and the final consonant blends in brackets should be in boxes.*

1. *cr* ab
2. *sk* u [nk]
3. c ō [lt]
4. *sw* ī ne
5. a [nt]
6. wh ā le
7. b ē e
8. fi sh
9. m ū le
10. e [lk]
11. *tr* ē e
12. *tw* ig
13. p ē a ch
14. *gr* ā pe
15. l ē af
16. *pl* um
17. *tr* u [nk]
18. *gr* ass
19. b ē et
20. v ī ne

21. m ē
22. J ō e
23. R ā y
24. J ō an
25. sh ē
26. Di ck
27. Be th
28. h ē
29. Ja ck
30. ch ī [ld]

31. w ā it
32. *st* a [nd]
33. *pr* ā y
34. *gr* ō w
35. *sc* ō [ld]
36. si ng
37. l ī e
38. *scr* ē am
39. h ō pe
40. ye [lp]

Gradebook: 87 points for the entire lesson

EXTRA ACTIVITY

"Print the words from page 64 (middle) in alphabetical order." You may want to have the children alphabetize the words from 64 (bottom) as well, giving some direction for the two words beginning with *w*.

TEST

Administer the unit test as part of Lesson 30 or as the total phonics activity on a separate day.

ANSWER KEY

A. *d* o g, *y* ar *n*, *p* ea *ch*, *b* o *x*
f i *sh*, *th* u *m* b, *v* a *s* e,
wh ea *t*

B. h *a* t, r *u* g, sh *i* p, n *e* st,
s *o* ck

C.
t – v	p – r	c – e
f – h	a – c	h – j
x – z	n – p	u – w
k – m	d – f	r – t

D.
1. *c* ast
2. tru *ck*
3. *c* ube
4. *k* ind
5. *k* eep
6. clo *ck*
7. soa *k*
8. *c* ot
9. ne *ck*
10. *k* it
11. *c* age
12. lea *k*

E.
1. te *ll*
2. hai *l*
3. gu *ll*
4. do *ll*
5. cu *ff*
6. sti *ff*
7. bee *f*
8. lea *f*

9. pa *ss*
10. ki *ss*
11. gee *s* e
12. le *ss*
13. bu *zz*
14. ga *z* e
15. fi *zz*
16. snee *z* e

F.
1.
2.
3.
4.
5.

ay
yw
sh
to
tr

Gradebook: 78 test points

Unit 2

UNIT 2
General Plan

Unit 2 reviews the variant vowels, consonants with more than one sound, silent letters, and suffixes studied in grade one.

More phonics terms are taught as well as practice in reading and printing pronunciation symbols.

Remove and file the tests for Units 2 and 3 from the back of the workbooks before distributing them.

Phonics Lessons   Unit 2

LESSON 1
The Digraph *oo*

A. The Sounds of *oo*—*workbook, page 6*

Ask the children what the pictures are at the top of the page. Have them tell you what vowel sound they hear in each word. Examine the word beside each picture and note that the vowel sound is spelled with *oo*. Tell the children that a macron over the two *o*'s indicates the long sound of *oo*—/ōō/. The two *o*'s with no mark represent the short sound—/oo/.

Let the children list words with the /ōō/ sound and then words with the /oo/ sound. If you think the class will need the help with the workbook page, print the words on the board as the children suggest them. Give clues to help them think of words until you have included all the words that will be needed for the sentences on the page. Then have them refer to that list for their answers.

B. Spellings for /ōō/ and /oo/—*workbook, page 7*

Let the children say the words given in the pronunciations on the page. Have them spell some of the words orally, using the spelling given for the digraph, or let them print some samples on the board for practice.

Review the rule for using *c* and *k* before certain vowels and remind the children to be careful to spell the words correctly that have the /k/ sound.

Review the rule for double consonants at the end of short vowel words.

ANSWER KEY

Page 6 (top)
1. pool
2. food
3. spoon
4. cool
5. bloom
6. Soon
7. moon

Page 6 (bottom)
1. cook
2. book
3. Look
4. good
5. took

Page 7 (top)
1. chew   4. drew
2. flew   5. grew
3. threw   6. screw

Page 7 (second part)
7. blue   9. true
8. glue   10. clue

Page 7 (third part)
1. put   4. full
2. push   5. bush
3. pull   6. bull

Page 7 (bottom) *Individual work.*

LESSON 2
Diphthongs

A. The Diphthong /oi/—*workbook, page 8*

Have the children identify the vowel sounds for the pictures at the top of the page, and discuss the rules for spelling the /oi/ sound. Pronounce words with the /oi/ sound for the children to tell you whether they would be spelled with *oi* or *oy*.

B. The Diphthong /ou/—*workbook, page 9*

Discuss the pictures and rules at the top of the page. Do the first exercise on the page orally for practice before assigning the written work.

ANSWER KEY

Page 8 (top)

1. p *oi* nt
2. j *oi* n
3. R *oy*
4. j *oi* nt
5. t *oy*
6. j *oy*
7. m *oi* st
8. s *oy*
9. b *oi* l
10. s *oi* l
11. *oi* l
12. b *oy*

Page 8 (bottom)

1. boy
2. joint
3. boil
4. Roy
5. soil
6. moist
7. joy

Page 9 (top)

1. l *ou* d
2. h *ow* l
3. c *ou* nt
4. c *ow*
5. gr *ow* l
6. cr *ow* n

7. n *ow*
8. f *ou* nd
9. br *ow* n
10. fr *ow* n
11. h *ou* se
12. *ow* l
13. t *ow* n
14. pr *ou* d
15. s *ou* r
16. h *ow*
17. sh *ou* t
18. p *ou* t

Page 9 (bottom)

1. house / town
2. town
3. sour
4. how
5. count
6. growl, howl

A diphthong is **two** vowel sounds in one **syllable**.

LESSON 3
Modified Vowel: ėr

A. We All Say /ėr/—*workbook, page 10*

Teach the ė symbol for the vowel sound of *i*, *e*, or *u* followed by *r*. It is difficult to separate the vowel sound from the /r/ sound and *r* may be printed with the vowel symbol as a unit.

Have the children spell some of the words from each section orally as you discuss the spelling.

B. The Sound of *or* after *w*—*workbook, page 11*

Ask the children which letters spell the /ẻr/ sound. After reviewing *er*, *ir*, and *ur*, they should be able to gather from page 11 that *or* says /ẻr/ and in which case it does so.

ANSWER KEY

Page 10 (first part)

1. her	4. term
2. fern	5. perch
3. herb	6. stern

Page 10 (second part)

1. girl	6. firm
2. dirt	7. shirt
3. first	8. bird
4. stir	9. chirp
5. birth	10. third

Page 10 (third part)

1. bur	4. burn
2. turn	5. burp
3. hurt	6. fur

Page 10 (bottom) *These are possible sentences.*

The bird has a nest in the ferns.
The girl scrubbed the dirt off the shirt.

Page 11 (top)

1. c
2. g
3. b
4. e
5. f
6. a
7. d

Page 11 (bottom)

1. worse
2. worry
3. worst
4. words
5. worms
6. work
7. worth

A modified vowel is ***changed*** by *r*.

A diphthong is two ***vowel sounds*** in one syllable.

EXTRA ACTIVITY

Let the children copy from the workbook some /ẻr/ words, placing two blanks in each word for the /ẻr/ sound. Then have them close their workbooks and see if they can remember which spelling to use in each word and print the letters in the blanks.

LESSON 4
Modified Vowels: är, ôr

A. Using *ar* and *or*—*workbook, page 12*

Have the children identify the vowel sounds for the pictures at the top of the page. Let them list other words containing the same sounds. Print them on the board if you think the class will need help with the sentences on the page. Give clues to help them to think of all the words that will be used in the sentences.

B. Diphthong Review—*workbook, page 13*

Review the rules for spelling the diphthongs.

ANSWER KEY

Page 12

1. M *ar* k, *ar* m
2. c *ar* ds, f *or*
3. st *ar* ted, *ar* t
4. C *ar* l, f *ar* m, c *ar* d
5. c *or* n, F *or* d
6. f *or* k, b *ar* n
7. D *ar* vin, c *ar* t
8. st *ar* s, c *ar* d
9. L *or* d, *ar* m
10. C *ar* la, j *ar*
11. y *ar* n, c *ar* d
12. h *ar* d, *ar* k, c *ar* d

Page 13 (top)

1. j *oi* n
2. j *oi* nt
3. s *oy*
4. j *oy*
5. sp *oi* l
6. R *oy*
7. v *oi* ce
8. c *oi* n
9. *oi* l
10. s *oi* l
11. b *oy*
12. c *oi* l
13. t *oy*
14. enj *oy*
15. h *oi* st
16. *oi* nk
17. destr *oy*
18. n *oi* se

Page 13 (bottom)

1. st *ou* t
2. o *ur*
3. dr *ow* n
4. *ou* t
5. br *ow*
6. b *ow*
7. m *ou* se
8. v *ow*
9. d *ow* n
10. l *ou* d
11. sc *ow* l
12. p *ou* nd
13. pr *ou* d
14. n *ow*
15. f *ow* l
16. m *ou* th
17. br *ow* n
18. fl *ou* r
19. c *ou* ch
20. *ow* l
21. fr *ow* n

A modified vowel is changed by *r*. A *diphthong* is two vowel sounds in one syllable.

Gradebook: 67 points in the entire lesson

EXTRA ACTIVITY

Let the children make the drawing suggested by the last sentence on page 12, or have them make cards for someone they know who is ill.

LESSON 5
Review

A. Modified Vowels and *oo*—workbook, page 14

Review the phonetic symbols for /ėr/, /ôr/, and /är/.

Print some samples on the board for the children to practice printing the respelling. Have them put the respelling in parenthesis to help keep the distinction between correct spelling and pronunciation.

Pronounce some words for the children to identify the /oo/ or /ōo/ sound. You may have them respond orally or in printing.

B. Dipththongs—*workbook, page 15*
Review the rules for spelling the diphthongs.
Drill the terms *digraph, diphthong,* and *modified vowel.*

ANSWER KEY

Page 14 (top)

1. (vėrs)	9. (bärk)
2. (wėrth)	10. (skėrt)
3. (pôrk)	11. (hėr)
4. (snôrt)	12. (nėrs)
5. (wėrd)	13. (fôrm)
6. (chėrch)	14. (smärt)
7. (thėrd)	15. (yärd)
8. (wėrm)	16. (pärt)

Page 14 (bottom) *Words in bold print should be circled.*

1. *took*, tōols, rōom
2. *good, wood*
3. stōol, rōom
4. rōof
5. sōon, *cook*, nōon
6. *look, foot*
7. brōom

Page 15 (top)

1. R *oy*, Ler *oy*, gr *ou* nd, h *ou* se
2. sh *ou* t, n *oi* se, ab *ou* t
3. b *oy* s, f *ou* nd
4. c *oi* ns
5. h *ow*
6. m *ou* se
7. b *oy* s, c *ou* nt, am *ou* nt

Page 15 (bottom)

1. A digraph is two letters together that make one sound.
2. A diphthong is two vowel sounds in one syllable.
3. A modified vowel is changed by *r.*

LESSON 6
Variant Vowel: ô

A. Spelled With *o*—*workbook, page 16*

Have the children read the sentence for the picture at the top of the page and identify the vowel sound. Teach them to make the circumflex over the *o.* Discuss respelling principles such as using *k* for all /k/ sounds and printing just one letter to represent the sound spelled with double consonants.

If in your locality, no difference is made in the pronunciation of *caught* and *cot,* you may want to alter the teaching of this page. Explain that some people say these words with a different sound, but in our area we say them just like the short *o* sound. Then have the children use an unmarked *o* in printing the pronunciations. You may tell the children which word to match with the ô symbol or let them use *o* and *ô* interchangeably in the matching exercise.

B. Spelled With *a*—*workbook, page 17*
Have the children read the word lists orally.

ANSWER KEY

Page 16 (top)

1. (fôg)	6. (kôst)
2. (strông)	7. (sông)
3. (môs)	8. (môth)
4. (lôst)	9. (sôft)
5. (tôs)	10. (frôst)

Page 16 (bottom)

1. hop
2. cross
3. no
4. good
5. do

ō
o
ô
ōō
oo

6. push
7. clock
8. wrong
9. threw
10. throw

ō
o
ô
ōō
oo

A diphthong is two vowel sounds in one **syllable**.
A modified **vowel** is changed by *r*.

Page 17 (top)

h **aw** k	l **aw** n	dr **aw**	has
y **aw** n	land	f **aw** n	crab
last	str **aw**	s **aw**	cr **aw** l

Page 17 (second part)

P **au** l	flat	had	l **au** d
Sam	f **au** lt	h **au** l	**au** to
S **au** l	**Au** gust	land	h **au** nt

Page 17 (third part)

t **a** ll	ch **a** lk	b **a** ll	f **a** ll
tack	sm **a** ll	smash	flat
w **a** lk	h **a** lt	hat	s **a** lt
c **a** ll	st **a** lk	w **a** ll	t **a** lk

Page 17 (bottom) *Individual work.*

LESSON 7
Suffixes: s, es

A. To Pluralize—*workbook, page 18*
Discuss the principle of adding *s* to make a word mean more than one. Review the rule of adding *es* to words that end with *x, s, sh* or *ch*. You may have the children circle those letters at the end of the words on the bottom of the page for a guide in printing the words.

B. For Verb Agreement—*workbook, page 19*
Print these sentences on the board for oral practice in understanding the directions.

I like to paint the wagon.
We wash the dirt off first.
You let the wagon dry.
We mix the paint with a stick.

I dip the brush carefully.
You brush the paint evenly.
We clean the brush after painting.

ANSWER KEY

Page 18 (top)

1. buns	6. figs
2. apples	7. cakes
3. peas	8. pears
4. beans	9. chips
5. pies	10. beets

Page 18 (bottom)

1. boxes	10. benches
2. sashes	11. foxes
3. grasses	12. chests
4. chairs	13. couches
5. glasses	14. brushes
6. switches	15. dresses
7. desks	16. beds
8. taxes	17. bushes
9. dishes	18. clocks

Page 19 (top)

1. He (she) fixes the meal.
2. He (she) sits at the table.
3. He (she) thanks God.
4. He (she) passes the food.
5. He (she) munches the crackers.
6. He (she) drinks the punch.
7. He (she) washes the dishes.

Page 19 (bottom)

1. end
2. diphthong
3. modified

EXTRA ACTIVITIES

1. Let the children classify the words listed in the first exercise on page 18 and list more words that fit in the same class. (food)

2. Have the children find and list the words from the second exercise on page 18 that name household furnishings.

LESSON 8
Suffixes: ed, ing

A. Sounds of *ed*—*workbook, page 20*

Discuss the examples at the top of the page with the children. Say words for them to identify the sound they hear for the suffix *ed*.

B. Review—*workbook, page 21*

Review the rule for adding *s* or *es*.

Have the children practice some of the numbers orally, noting the number of syllables as they say the words.

ANSWER KEY

Page 20 (top)

1. wailed (d)	5. talked (t)
2. bawled (d)	6. hinted (ed)
3. asked (t)	7. called (d)
4. scolded (ed)	8. chirped (t)

Page 20 (bottom)

1. weeding	6. cleaning
2. cooking	7. planting
3. sawing	8. washing
4. mending	9. building
5. plowing	10. painting

Page 21

1. wishes   wished   wishing
2. waxes   waxed   waxing
3. plays   played   playing
4. splashes   splashed   splashing
5. presses   pressed   pressing
6. pinches   pinched   pinching
7. helps   helped   helping
8. misses   missed   missing

Suffixes are letters added at the end of words.

Gradebook: 51 points for the entire lesson

EXTRA ACTIVITIES

1. Classify the words in the first exercise on page 20 and think of more words that fit in the same class. (manner of speaking)

2. Sort the words in the second exercise of page 20 into two groups—work Father does, and work Mother does.

LESSON 9
Suffixes: y, ly

A. The Suffix *y*—*workbook, page 22*

Print these words on the board for the children to add the letter *y*. Have them say the original word and the word they have after the *y* is added.

     crumb   bump   mist   lump
     wind   rain   crust   smell

You may want to have the children do a few of the sentences orally to help them to understand the directions.

B. The Suffix *ly*—*workbook, page 23*

Let the children add *ly* to these words and pronounce both forms, noting the number of syllables.

     kind   free   sure   soft
     hard   nice   bad   poor

ANSWER KEY

Page 22

1. dusty
2. salty
3. trashy
4. sleepy
5. squeaky
6. cloudy
7. rocky
8. stretchy
9. sticky
10. jumpy
11. rusty
12. milky

Page 23

1. gladly
2. sweetly
3. tightly
4. sadly
5. swiftly
6. nightly
7. smoothly
8. brightly
9. quickly
10. wisely
11. slowly
12. strangely

Suffixes are **letters** added at the **end** of **words**.

LESSON 10
Root Words and Syllables

A. Identifying Root Words—*workbook, page 24*

Review the various suffixes the children have studied. Tell the children that a word that does not have any parts added is called a root word. Print some sets of words on the board such as *help—helping, sand—sandy,* and have the children tell you which is the root word. Print some words with suffixes and have the children circle the root words in them.

B. Syllables and Review of Terms—*workbook, page 25*

Have the children read the lists orally, noting that the suffix does not always add a syllable to the pronunciation.

ANSWER KEY

Page 24 (top)

1. slow	7. sing
2. dirt	8. box
3. wash	9. dish
4. sure	10. finish
5. print	11. paper
6. jump	12. frog

Page 24 (bottom)

1. *cold* ly, *blow* ing, *boy* s
2. *gather* ing, *bunch* es, *carrot* s
3. *pack* ed, *box* es
4. *health* y, *snack* s, *lunch* es
5. *hand* ed, *boy* s, *crunch* y, *help* ing, *nice* ly

Page 25 (top)

1. 1	9. 1	17. 1
2. 2	10. 1	18. 1
3. 1	11. 1	19. 1
4. 2	12. 1	20. 2
5. 2	13. 1	21. 1
6. 2	14. 2	22. 2
7. 1	15. 2	23. 1
8. 2	16. 3	24. 2

Page 25 (bottom)

1. d
2. e
3. g
4. b
5. a
6. f
7. c

EXTRA ACTIVITY

Have the children look in the reader for words that have suffixes. Let them copy the words and circle the root word in each one.

LESSON 11
Vowels: w, y

**A. The Vowel *y*—*workbook, page 26*

Discuss each of the situations in which *y* is a vowel. Give some samples and let the children list additional ones.

Note the directions for the last five sentences. The children are to find all the words in which *y* is a vowel, including those which fit the rules for the first two exercises on the page.

B. The Vowel *w*—workbook, page 27

Discuss the situations in which *w* is a vowel and let the children give examples for each one.

Tell the children to be careful with the *y*'s and *w*'s at the bottom of the page. Some of them are consonants.

ANSWER KEY

Page 26 (top)

a, e, i, o, u

Page 26 (second part)
1. try, my
2. fry
3. Why, shy, cry
4. by

Page 26 (third part)
5. surely, many, happy
6. sunny, cheery
7. cloudy, chilly, windy
8. lovingly, every

Page 26 (bottom)
9. say, may, boy
10. toy
11. my, gray
12. happy, play
13. sky, stormy, yesterday, today

Page 27 (top)
1. grow, grew
2. blow, blew
3. Throw, threw
4. crawl, lawn
5. claw, jaw

Page 27 (middle)
6. How, down
7. growl, cow
8. howls, owl
9. crowds, town

Page 27 (bottom)

1. aw	6. ew	11. ay	16. y
2. ea	7. y	12. ow	17. oy
3. i y	8. ow	13. ew	18. i e
4. ow	9. oy	14. u y	19. ay
5. ay	10. ou	15. ow	20. aw

EXTRA ACTIVITY

Have the children find and put an *x* on all the *y*'s that are consonants on page 26.

LESSON 12
Sounds of *s*

A. Sounds of *s*—workbook, page 28

To focus on the sounds of *s*, have the children underline the *s* in a word, then try pronouncing it with both the /s/ and the /z/ sound.

Review respelling principles such as using vowel markings, *k* for all /k/ sounds, and one letter for double consonants.

B. Review—*workbook, page 29*

Print these words on the board for practice. Let the children find the root words, and then use each root word with another suffix.

rained   friendly   rooms

Ask the children for oral samples of each of the items in the last part of the page.

ANSWER KEY

Page 28 (top)

1. (s)	6. (s)	11. (s)
2. (s)	7. (z)	12. (z)
3. (z)	8. (s)	13. (s)
4. (s)	9. (s)	14. (z)
5. (s)	10. (z)	15. (s)

Page 28 (bottom)

1. (az)	9. (iz)
2. (pas)	10. (les)
3. (sok)	11. (sôrt)
4. (wīz)	12. (sōp)
5. (stärz)	13. (thėrst)
6. (dāz)	14. (sed)
7. (sô)	15. (chōōz)
8. (nėrs)	16. (plēz)

Page 29 (top)

1. hand   hands / handed handing
2. trust   trusty / trusting

3. year   years
4. punch   punched / punching
5. sound   sounds / sounded soundly

Page 29 (middle)

1. ball   oo   6. should   oo
2. boot   oo   7. shoe   oo
3. book   oi   8. joy————oi
4. boy   ou   9. jaw   ou
5. bound   ô   10. shout   ô

Page 29 (bottom) *Individual work.*

Gradebook: 34 points for page 29

EXTRA ACTIVITY

Let capable students try to print pronunciations for the words at the top of page 28.

LESSON 13
Sounds of *c* and *y*

**A. Sounds of *c*—*workbook, page 30*

Discuss the rule at the top of the page and help the children to realize that doing the first item in the directions will tell them the answers in the second step.

**B. Sounds of *y*—*workbook, page 31*

Review the cases in which *y* is a vowel.

ANSWER KEY

Page 30

1. ce (s)	9. (k)	17. ci (s)		17. red	25. green
2. ce (s)	10. ci (s)	18. (k)		18. yellow	26. green
3. (k)	11. cy (s)	19. cy (s)		19. green	27. red
4. cy (s)	12. ce (s)	20. (k)		20. red	28.
5. ce (s)	13. (k)	21. ci (s)		21.	29. green
6. (k)	14. ci (s)	22 (k)		22. yellow	30. yellow
7. cy (s)	15. ce (s)	23. cy (s)		23.	31.
8. (k)	16. (k)	24. (k)		24. yellow	32. green

Page 31 (bottom)
Individual work.

Page 31 *The letter y should have colored spots.*

1. yellow	9.
2. red	10. green
3.	11. red
4. green	12. green
5. yellow	13. yellow
6. yellow	14. green
7. red	15. yellow
8. yellow	16. red

C says /s/ when it comes before *e,* *i,* or *y*.

EXTRA ACTIVITY

Have the children tell the number of syllables in the words on page 31.

LESSON 14
Sounds of *g*

A. Sounds of *g*—*workbook, page 32*
Discuss the rule and directions given at the top of the page.

B. Review—*workbook, page 33*
Discuss these rules for printing pronunciations:
    a. Use *z* for *s* when it has the /z/ sound.
    b. Use *j* for *g* when it has the /j/ sound.
    c. Use *s* or *k* for *c*.
    d. Mark long vowels with a macron.
    e. Do not print silent letters.
    f. Use the ô symbol if you have taught it.
Drill the rules for soft *g* and *c*.

ANSWER KEY

Page 32 (top)

1.	(g)	9. ge	(j)	17. ge	(j)
2. gi	(j)	10.	(g)	18. gy	(j)
3.	(g)	11. gi	(j)	19.	(g)
4. ge	(j)	12. ge	(j)	20.	(g)
5. ge	(j)	13. ge	(j)	21. gi	(j)
6.	(g)	14.	(g)	22.	(g)
7. ge	(j)	15. gy	(j)	23. ge	(j)
8. gy	(j)	16.	(g)	24.	(g)

Page 32 (bottom)

Individual work.

Page 33 (top)

1. (haz)	9. (sôlt)
2. (nōz)	10. (fãs)
3. (sāv)	11. (rīs)
4. (fens)	12. (klô)
5. (jem)	13. (kub)
6. (gōt)	14. (kūt)
7. (yel)	15. (pik)
8. (sām)	16. (grēn)

Page 33 (middle)

1. 2	7. 1	13. 3
2. 3	8. 2	14. 3
3. 1	9. 3	15. 2
4. 2	10. 2	16. 2
5. 2	11. 3	17. 3
6. 2	12. 3	18. 3

Page 33 (bottom)

G says /j/ when it comes before *e,*
   i, or *y.*

C says /*s*/ when it comes ***before***
   e, i, or y.

EXTRA ACTIVITY

Have the children print the root words for the words that have suffixes in the second exercise on page 33.

LESSON 15
Silent Letters: *k*n, *w*r, Final *e*

A. Silent Consonants—*workbook, page 34*

Discuss the examples at the top of the page with the children.

Review some points on printing pronunciations.

a. Do not print silent letters.

b. Mark long vowels with a macron.

B. Silent Vowels—*workbook, page 35*

Discuss the rules at the top of the page and teach the children to cross out each letter with a slash mark that goes through one letter only to make their answers clear.

Review the phonics terms used in the lower part of the page.

ANSWER KEY

Page 34 (top)

1. (nob)	4. (nō)	7. (rīt)	10. (nōō)
2. (nok)	5. (nīf)	8. (nēl)	11. (rench)
3. (ren)	6. (rōt)	9. (rap)	12. (rông)

Page 34 (bottom)
1. wren
2. wrap
3. wrench, knife
4. knew, wrong
5. knock, knob
6. write, wrote

Page 35 (top)
1. cav ¢
2. pil ¢
3. mul ¢
4. ra í d
5. ja ý
6. ti ¢ d
7. hom ¢
8. bik ¢
9. fe ¢ l
10. wo ¢

11. ston ¢
12. he á p
13. vin ¢
14. ma ý
15. kit ¢
16. lo w̸
17. go á t
18. wast ¢
19. di ¢
20. nam ¢

long

Page 35 (bottom)
1. diphthong
2. modified
3. suffix
4. root word
5. before
6. j, before

Gradebook: 50 points for the whole lesson

LESSON 16
Silent Letters: *gn, bu, gu*

A. Silent Consonants—*workbook, page 36*

Discuss the rule with the children. Explain that they will be able to match the words with the pronunciations by comparing the spelling even though they are unfamiliar words. They will need to match the words with the meanings by thinking about what the sentences say.

B. Silent Vowels—*workbook, page 37*

The letter *u* is usually silent after *b* or *g*, unless it is needed for the vowel sound of the syllable. Teach the children how to recognize whether the *u* will be silent by the spelling.

Have the children read the word lists orally after they have marked the vowels.

ANSWER KEY

Page 36 (top)	(middle)	(bottom)
1. gnat	1. gnaw	1. gnarl
2. gnu	2. gnu	2. gnu
3. gnaw	3 gnat	3. gnat
4. gnome	4. gnarl	4. gnome
5. gnarl	5. gnash	5. gnaw
6. gnash	6. gnome	6. gnash

Page 37 (middle)

b ~~u~~ *i* ld   bu *l* l
g u *l* l   g ~~u~~ *a* rd
g ~~u~~ *e* ss   gu *m*
b ~~u~~ *y* er   g ~~u~~ *i* le
gu *t* ter   b ~~u~~ *i* lds

bu *c* k   g ~~u~~ *i* lty
b ~~u~~ *y*   bu *b* ble
g ~~u~~ *i* lt   b ~~u~~ *o* y
gu *p* py   b ~~u~~ *i* lt
g ~~u~~ *i* de   bu *t* ter

Page 37 (bottom)

1. buy   7. guile
2. buoy   8. build
3. buyer   9. guilt
4. guide   10. built
5. guess   11. guilty
6. builds   12. guard

LESSON 17
Silent Consonants: *gn, bt, mb*

A. The Letters *gn, bt, mb*—*workbook, page 38*

Discuss the silent letter combinations at the top of the page and print these samples on the board for the children to practice pronouncing.

doubt   thumb   sign   lamb
signs   debt   bomb   doubts

Review the rules for silent vowels.

B. Context Clues—*workbook, page 39*

Encourage the children again to find out the word meanings by thinking about what the sentences say.

ANSWER KEY

Page 38 (top)

1. si ~~g~~ n   6. crum ~~b~~
2. lim ~~b~~   7. dou ~~b~~ ts
3. de ~~b~~ t   8. lam ~~b~~
4. si ~~g~~ ned   9. dou ~~b~~ ting
5. bom ~~b~~   10. clim ~~b~~

11. si ~~g~~ ns   16. dou ~~b~~ t
12. dum ~~b~~   17. plum ~~b~~
13. resi ~~g~~ n   18. thum ~~b~~
14. dou ~~b~~ ted   19. desi ~~g~~ n
15. com ~~b~~   20. de ~~b~~ ts

Page 38 (bottom)

1. lam ~~b~~   9. g ~~u~~ ilt
2. ~~k~~ ne ~~e~~ l   10. ~~w~~ rit ~~e~~
3. co ~~a~~ ch   11. ~~g~~ narl
4. si ~~g~~ n   12. spra ~~y~~
5. b ~~u~~ ilt   13. crum ~~b~~
6. ~~g~~ nom ~~e~~   14. flo ~~w~~
7. ~~w~~ re ~~a~~ th   15. ~~k~~ nob
8. tra ~~y~~   16. dou ~~b~~ t

17. ho ~~e~~
18. g~~u~~es~~s~~
19. de~~b~~ t
20. b~~u~~y
21. g~~u~~id ~~e~~
22. ti ~~e~~ d
23. thum ~~b~~
24. ~~w~~rot ~~e~~
25. re ~~a~~ ch
26. clim ~~b~~
27. ~~k~~nif ~~e~~
28. ~~g~~nat
29. cha ~~i~~ n
30. sho ~~w~~
31. si ~~g~~ ns
32. b ~~u~~ ild

Page 39 (middle)

1. sign
2. doubt
3. lamb
4. debt
5. jamb
6. design

Page 39 (bottom)

1. doubt
2. jamb
3. debt
4. sign
5. lamb
6. design

EXTRA ACTIVITY

Have the children print words from the lists at the bottom of page 38 with suffixes.

LESSON 18
Silent Letters: *l*f, *l*k, *l*m, *t*ch

A. The Letters *l*f, *l*k, *l*m, *t*ch—*workbook, page 40*

Discuss the silent-letter combinations at the top of the page and print samples for each one on the board for the children to cross out the silent letters and pronounce the words.

calf	chalk	palm	hitch
half	walk	calm	fetch

B. Review of Silent Letters—*workbook, page 41*

Have the children read the lists of pronunciations orally.

Let the children name the silent-letter combinations you have studied and print them on the board. See if the children can spell some of the words for the top of page 41 orally. Let them turn back to the previous lessons to help them get the correct spelling in the written work.

ANSWER KEY

Page 40 (top)

1. ca ~~l~~ m
2. clu ~~t~~ ch
3. ta ~~l~~ k
4. ha ~~l~~ f
5. wa ~~l~~ k
6. scra ~~t~~ ch
7. pa ~~l~~ m
8. di ~~t~~ ch
9. ca ~~l~~ f
10. stre ~~t~~ ch
11. sta ~~l~~ k
12. pa ~~t~~ ch
13. cha ~~l~~ k
14. fe ~~t~~ ch
15. ha ~~t~~ ch
16. ~~p~~ sa ~~l~~ m

Page 40 (bottom)
patch, calf, palm
stalk, ditch, half

Page 41 (top)

1. talk
2. hatch
3. walk
4. calm
5. half
6. sign
7. debt
8. wren
9. pitch
10. palm
11. calf
12. stitch
13. chalk
14. thumb
15. guess
16. knock

Page 41 (bottom)
Individual work.

LESSON 19
Silent Letters: *gh*

A. Words With *igh*—workbook, page 42

Tell the children that *i* has the long sound when followed by *gh* and have them read the word lists.

B. Other *gh* Words—workbook, page 43

Print these keys on the board, and then have the children practice reading the word lists.

eigh = ā
ough = ō or ô
augh = ô

ANSWER KEY

Page 42 (top)

hi gh	ti gh t
si gh	fri gh t
thi gh	sli gh t
bri gh t	ri gh t
fri gh t	bli gh t

ni gh t	midni gh t
fli gh t	li gh tning
mi gh t	fri gh ten
pli gh t	ti gh tness
mi gh ty	li gh tly

Page 42 (bottom)

1. right	5. frighten
2. tight	6. mighty
3. lightly	7. high
4. lightning	8. midnight

Page 43

1. daughter
2. weigh
3. thought
4. though
5. naughty
6. neighbor
7. eight
8. brought
9. sleigh
10. taught

Gradebook: 38 points for the whole lesson

LESSON 20
Review

A. Digraphs, Diphthongs, Modified Vowels, Suffixes—workbook, page 44

Review definitions and samples for each of the items in the directions. If necessary, take more than one day for this lesson to thoroughly review the terms and understandings.

You may wish to give the children the number of answers expected for each item. The *ey* in *they* is a vowel digraph. Do not expect the children to include it unless you teach it as a digraph and tell them to mark it as well.

You may also want to make special mention of the digraph *oo*, and *ou* as a digraph in the word *you*.

B. Silent Letters—*workbook, page 45*
Self-explanatory

ANSWER KEY

Page 44

a. *purple—21 consonant digraphs*
1. *Th* e
2. *th* e, bu *sh* es, ro *ck* s
3. si *ng*, bran *ch* es
4. *wh* ere, *th* ere, *sh* ade
5. *Wh* en, *th* ey
6.
7. Su *ch*, bloomi *ng*
8. *th* e, *th* e
9. bri *ng*, blowi *ng*
10. *th* ink, *th* e, *ch* ildren, *th* e

b. *blue—13 vowel digraphs (counting* ey *and* ou)
1.
2. b *ea* ts
3. pl *ay*
4.
5. th *ey*, cr *ee* p, s *ee* k, f *oo* d
6. r *ai* ned, bl *oo* m
7. bl *oo* ming, s *ee*
8.
9. bl *ow* ing
10. y *ou*, r *oa* med

c. *yellow—7 diphthongs*
1.
2. d *ow* n
3.
4.
5. *ou* t
6. fl *ow* ers
7. j *oy*
8. *oi* l, gr *ou* nd
9.
10. H *ow*

d. *green—14 modified vowels*
1. des *er* t
2.
3. B *ir* ds
4. Des *er* t
5. d *ar* k
6. Aft *er*, flow *er* s
7. *ar* e
8. des *er* t, f *or*, und *er*
9. Des *er* t, st *or* ms
10. f *ar*, des *er* t

e. *red—16 suffixes*
1. sand *y*
2. beat *s*, bush *es*, rock *s*
3. Bird *s*, branch *es*
4. animal *s*
5.
6. rain *ed*, flower *s*, plant *s*
7. bloom *ing*, plant *s*, sure *ly*
8.
9. storm *s*, blow *ing*
10. roam *ed*

Page 45
1. (sī)
2. (sīn)
3. (chôk)
4. (kōm)
5. (gilt)
6. (hī)
7. (rek)
8. (det)
9. (nēd)
10. (haf)
11. (nô)
12. (rōt)
13. (stich)
14. (no͞o)

15. (gīd)
16. (lim)
17. (bild)
18. (dout)
19. (nat)
20. (kôm)

EXTRA ACTIVITY

Let the children draw a picture to go with the sentences on page 44.

LESSON 21
Words With *ear, eer,*

A. Using *ear* and *eer*—*workbook, page 46*

Discuss the word endings at the top of the page and let the children go through the alphabet for initial consonants. Don't forget to try blends and digraphs as well.

If you think the children will need the help, you may want to print their words on the board, separating the spellings into two lists. Give clues until they have listed all the words that will be needed for the page.

B. Final Consonants—*workbook, page 47*

In class practice, see how many different words the children can make by adding different consonants to one word beginning.

ANSWER KEY

Page 46

1. *f* ear	8. *sp* ear
2. *d* eer	9. *st* eer
3. *ch* eer	10. *cl* ear
4. *n* ear	11. *sm* ear
5. *qu* eer	12. *p* eer
6. *y* ear	13. *h* ear
7. *d* ear	14. *b* eer

Page 47 (top) *Various answers are correct.*

Page 47 (bottom)

1. me *ss*
2. cu *ff*
3. ti *ll* / ti *ck*
4. ra *ck*
5. we *ll*
6. bu *zz* / bu *ll* / bu *ff* / bu *ck*
7. ba *ss* / ba *ll* / ba *ck*
8. sni *ff*
9. sho *ck*
10. mu *ss* / mu *ff* / mu *ck*
11. sa *ss* / sa *ck*
12. de *ck* / de *ll*
13. ro *ck*
14. pa *ss* / pa *ck*
15. fe *ll*
16. ki *ss* / ki *ll* / ki *ck*
17. lo *ss* / lo *ck*
18. whi *zz* / whi *ff*

EXTRA ACTIVITY

Let the children choose words from page 47 and list columns making as many words as they can for the same beginning.

LESSON 22
Words With *are, air, ear*

A. Using *are, air, ear*—*workbook, page 48*

Get the children to say each of these endings as /ār/ (or the pronunciation you prefer) rather than saying them as the words *are, air,* and *ear.*

Let the children go through the alphabet for initial consonants for the word endings. Also consider blends and digraphs.

If the children need the help for the workbook lesson, print the words they say on the board in lists according to the spelling.

B. Suffix Review—*workbook, page 49*

Review the rule for adding *s* or *es.*

Print these sample sentences on the board and have the children read them with an *ed* suffix as well as an *ing* suffix, to recognize the correct usage.

1. Aunt Sue call___ last night.
2. While Mother was talk___, we guessed she had exciting news.
3. The family that visit___ our church will move to our town.

ANSWER KEY

Page 48

1. **sh** are
2. **f** air
3. **st** are
4. **w** ear
5. **sc** are
6. **p** ear
7. **h** air
8. **ch** air
9. **b** ear
10. **p** air
11. **b** are
12. **t** ear
13. **squ** are
14. **st** airs

Page 49 (top)

1. s	8. es	15. es
2. es	9. s	16. es
3. s	10. es	17. s
4. s	11. es	18. es
5. es	12. s	19. s
6. s	13. es	20. es
7. es	14. s	21. s

Page 49 (bottom)

1. look **ing**
2. call **ed**
3. wonder **ed**
4. guess **ing**
5. join **ed**,   inspect **ing**
6. mark **ed**
7. touch **ed**
8. answer **ed**,   tell **ing**

EXTRA ACTIVITY

Have the children classify the words in the list at the top of page 49 and think of other words that fit in the same class. (words related to plants)

LESSON 23
Words With *oar, ear*

A. Using *oar*—*workbook, page 50*
Print some of the words on the board for the children to practice saying. Tell them to use the sentences to help them understand the meanings of the words for the second exercise.

B. Sounds of *ear*—*workbook, page 51*
Have the children read the word lists orally.

ANSWER KEY

Page 50 (top)
1. r *oar*
2. b *oar*
3. s *oar*
4. *oar*
5. h *oar*
6. h *oar* se
7. b *oar* d

Page 50 (bottom)
1. oar
2. roar
3. hoarse
4. boar
5. soar
6. board
7. hoar

Page 51 (bottom)
1. learn
2. hear
3. clear
4. fear
5. search
6. near
7. tear
8. earn
9. pear
10. year

EXTRA ACTIVITY
"Choose a verse from the Bible to copy and learn." You may want to suggest Psalm 119 or some other passage as a source.

LESSON 24
The Apostrophe

A. Possessives—*workbook, page 52*
Print samples on the board to teach the use of the apostrophe and *s*, and to give the children practice in printing the possessive form.

B. All *s* Endings—*workbook, page 53*
Print the following sentences on the board to consider the different *s* endings.
1. Four card___ came in the mail for Sara.
2. It was Sara___ birthday.
3. She found two little box___ on the table when she came home from school.
4. Her brother___ had made some furniture for her doll house.

It may help the children to recognize the possessive words if they underline the phrase including the name and the thing owned each time they think an apostrophe should be used.

ANSWER KEY

Page 52 (top) *An apostrophe and* s *should be added in each blank.*

Page 52 (bottom) *Any names may be used ending with* 's.

Page 53
1. rabbit *s*
2. rabbit *s*
3. Earl *'s*
4. lamb *'s*, father *'s*

5. Seth *'s*
6. Cindy *'s*
7. Cindy *'s*, finger *s*
8. fox *es*
9. pet *s*, time *s*
10. bird *s*
11. shoulder *s*, dish *es*
12. boy *s*, girl *s*, pet *s*

Gradebook: 24 points for page 52

LESSON 25
Review

A. Syllables and Suffixes—*workbook, page 54*
Do some oral practice in class, letting the children say the words with as many suffixes as they can.

B. Adding *s* Endings—*workbook, page 55 (top)*
Review the use of *'s* and practice again the distinction of plurals and possessives, using these sample sentences:
  1. Peter___ trousers and shoe___ were muddy.
  2. His shirt was torn, and his arm___ had scratch___.
  3. How will he answer Mother___ question___?

C. Phonics Terms—*workbook, page 55 (bottom)*
Review the definitions of the phonics terms.

ANSWER KEY

Page 54 *Varied answers are given.*

1.	2			6.	2	
offered	2	4.	1	witnessed	2	
offering	3	thirsted	2	witnessing	3	
2.	2	thirsting	2	7.	2	
coveted	3	thirsty	2	honored	2	
coveting	3	5.	2	honoring	3	
3.	1	traveled	2	8.	1	
thickly	2	traveling	3	softly	2	

9.   1
   tempted   2
   tempting   2
10.   1
   sweetly   2
11.   1
   healthy   2
12.   3
   importantly 4

Page 55 (top)
1. mother *'s*, helper *s*
2. bedroom *s*
3. shirt *s*, dress *es*
4. Linda *'s*
5. Kathy *'s*, floor *s*
6. broom *s*, brush *es*
7. Allen *'s*, window *s*

Page 55 (bottom)
1. diphthong
2. modified
3. e, i, y

4. vowels
5. sound
6. suffix
7. belongs

Gradebook: 21 points for page 55

EXTRA ACTIVITY
   Print a list of words such as the following on the board and have the children use them in phrases, first as plurals and then as possessives.

boy	bird
girl	father
fox	bush
cat	clock
duck	flower
bus	finch

Example: five *boys*
        boy's room
        two *birds*
        bird's feathers

LESSON 26
Words With *le*

A. Recognizing Pronunciations—*workbook, page 56*
   Explain the use of the apostrophe as a symbol for the vowel sound. The vowel sound in these syllables is so indistinct that we do not use a letter to represent the sound. Pronounce some *le* syllables for the children and let them practice the pronunciations.

B. Printing Pronunciations—*workbook, page 57*
   Pronounce some *le* words for the children to print the pronunciations on the board, giving the two syllables slowly and distinctly. Teach them to put a dot between the two syllables of the pronunciation.

ANSWER KEY

Page 56 (top)

1. c	6. g
2. b	7. f
3. a	8. i
4. d	9. j
5. e	10. h

Page 56 (bottom)

1. table	5. simple
2. sample	6. stumble
3. turtle	7. tremble
4. title	8. trample

Page 57 (top)

1. (thim·b'l)
2. (dim·p'l)
3. (stär·t'l)
4. (man·t'l)
5. (han·d'l)
6. (pėr·p'l)
7. (bun·d'l)
8. (mär·b'l)
9. (kan·d'l)
10. (grum·b'l)
11. (krum·b'l)
12. (krum·p'l)
13. (jen·t'l)
14. (tram·p'l)

Page 57 (bottom)
Individual work.

EXTRA ACTIVITY
Let the children make pictures for their original sentences.

LESSON 27
Suffixes: er, est

A. Using er and est—*workbook, page 58*

Let the children practice adding the suffixes orally to these words:

cold	warm	fast	fresh
small	low	soft	hungry
busy	lazy	round	angry

Let the children tell you which word they will use from the first sentence to finish the other sentences in some of the groups.

B. Syllables and le Endings—*workbook, page 59*

Have the children read the word lists for the top of the page orally to see if they can read the words which have had *y* changed to *i* to add a suffix.

Let them spell some of the *le* words orally to review the spelling of the second syllable.

ANSWER KEY

Page 58

1. b. longer c. longest
2. b. higher c. highest
3. b. thicker c. thickest
4. b. stronger c. strongest
5. b. sweeter c. sweetest

Page 59 (top)

1. 2	8. 1	15. 2
2. 2	9. 3	16. 1
3. 2	10. 2	17. 3
4. 1	11. 2	18. 2
5. 2	12. 3	19. 3
6. 2	13. 2	20. 2
7. 3	14. 3	21. 1

Page 59 (bottom)

1. stumble	7. dimple
2. sample	8. bundle
3. startle	9. grumble
4. tremble	10. gentle
5. handle	11. trample
6. marble	12. candle

EXTRA ACTIVITY

Print these words on the board and have the children copy them and add the *er* and *est* form for each one.

kind	short
long	light
mean	deep
cool	pink

LESSON 28
Suffixes: less, ful

A. Adding Suffixes—*workbook, page 60*

Discuss the meaning of the suffixes. Let the children do some of the exercises orally and discover that many of the words may have either suffix added.

B. Printing Words by Meaning—*workbook, page 61*

Teach the children that *full* has just one *l* when used as a suffix. Let them give orally the words for these definitions and for the exercise on page 61 if you wish.

without sugar	full of joy
full of sorrow	without bones
without a job	full of wonder
without clouds	without a tune

ANSWER KEY

Page 60

1. endless
2. painless / painful
3. sinless / sinful
4. handful
5. faithless / faithful
6. thankless / thankful

7. helpless / helpful
8. armless / armful
9. cheerless / cheerful
10. homeless
11. harmless / harmful
12. thoughtless / thoughtful

Page 61

1. hopeless	8. useful
2. hopeful	9. shameless
3. careless	10. shameful
4. careful	11. fearless
5. doubtless	12. fearful
6. doubtful	13. powerless
7. useless	14. powerful

EXTRA ACTIVITY

Have the children print sentences with some of the pairs of words from page 61.

LESSON 29
Compound Words

A. Dividing Compounds—*workbook, page 62*

Discuss the definition of *compound word*. Print these samples on the board for the children to practice dividing by drawing a vertical line between the two words.

barefoot	baseball	doorway
butterfly	schoolmate	bookend
birdhouse	rainbow	housefly
mailman	snowball	airplane

B. Making Compounds—*workbook, page 63*

Print these lists on the board and let the children match words to make compounds. Encourage various combinations.

day	room
bed	light
bath	house
dog	yard
farm	stool
foot	step

ANSWER KEY

Page 62

1.
2. dog   house
3. gate   way
4. snow   flake
5. sail   boat
6. mail   box
7. sky   light
8. sun   shine
9. blue   bird
10. butter   milk

11. pan   cake
12. foot   ball
13. book   case
14. door   bell

Page 63

1. yardstick
2. rosebud
3. starfish
4. snowman
5. bedroom
6. teakettle
7. grasshopper
8. toothpick

Gradebook: 21 points for the whole lesson

LESSON 30
More Compound Words

A. Dividing words—*workbook, page 64*

Have the children read the word list at the top of the page.

B. Review—*workbook, page 65*

If the children think they do not know the words in the list at the top of page 65, tell them to look for two words in each word.

Review definitions of the phonics terms used on the bottom of the page.

ANSWER KEY

Page 64 (top)

foot / steps	flash / light	night / time
some / where	every / thing	over / coat
farm / yard	rail / road	mail / man
hand / bag	up / stairs	play / house

Page 64 (bottom)
1. nighttime
2. farmyard
3. overcoat
4. flashlight
5. upstairs
6. somewhere, footsteps
7. everything

Page 65 (top)

1. 2	6. 2	11. 3
2. 2	7. 4	12. 3
3. 2	8. 2	13. 2
4. 3	9. 3	14. 2
5. 3	10. 3	15. 2

Page 65 (bottom)
Individual work.

EXTRA ACTIVITY

Have the children print the two words they find in each of the compound words at the top of page 65, and print the number of syllables in each of those words. They can do a bit of arithmetic to check the answers they wrote in the book for the number of syllables in the compound words.

TEST

ANSWER KEY

A.
1. *er*   sing
2. *ed*   pray
3. *y*   storm
4. *ful*   care
5. *est*   great

6. *ing*   sleep
7. *ly*   friend
8. *less*   seed
9. *ful*   joy
10. *ly*   cost

B.
1. robin *'s*
2. bush *es*
3. egg *s*
4. Carol *'s*
5. branch *es*
6. bird *s*

C.
1. ca l m
2. dou b t
3. w rot e
4. ha l f
5. g u ilt

6. g nat
7. b u ild
8. lim b
9. g nash
10. com b

11. hi gh
12. sti t ch
13. g u id e
14. k no w
15. si g n

D.
1. blend
2. digraph
3. diphthong
4. modified
5. suffix
6. compound
7. 's
8. gh

Gradebook: 53 test points, counting one point for each silent letter in part C

Unit 3

UNIT 3
General Plan

In Unit 3 the children study rules for adding suffixes to words and some principles of syllabication. The accent mark, schwa, and breve are introduced as pronunciation symbols. Although the breve is not used as a standard symbol in this series, familiarity with the symbol is an advantage when using various dictionaries.

Phonics Lessons   Unit 3

LESSON 1
Doubling Consonants to Add Suffixes

Doubling Consonants—*workbook, pages 68 and 69*

Do the following exercise with the children in their workbooks or using samples printed on the board.

First have them identify and circle the suffixes they see. Then have them circle the root words, being sure to circle only the letters that are in the root word at the beginning of each line. It will then be evident that there is an extra letter in the word when it is written with a suffix. Discuss the questions on the page with the class or have the students do them on their own.

Have several children read the bold print rule, and then have the class read it together. Say the rule and let the class fill in the words that are in italics. To help them realize that the rule applies to the words they will be printing in the exercises, call attention to certain numbers in the exercises, and ask if the word has a short vowel, one ending consonant, and only one syllable.

ANSWER KEY

Page 68 (top)

1. yes
2. yes
3. yes
4. yes

Page 68 (bottom)

1. wetter
2. bidder
3. dimmer
4. bragger
5. shopper
6. scrubber

Page 69

7. wettest
8. biggest
9. hottest
10. flattest
11. thinnest
12. drabbest

13. fanning
14. rubbing
15. stepping
16. plotting
17. dripping
18. shutting
19. penned
20. tapped
21. robbed
22. trimmed
23. shrugged
24. slammed
25. foggy
26. muddy
27. stubby
28. floppy
29. tinny
30. shaggy

LESSON 2
When to Double Consonants

Using the Rule—*workbook, pages 70 and 71*

Review the rule from Lesson 1. Print the following list of words on the board. Let the children find the words to which the rule applies and have them print those words on the board with the suffixes that you tell them to use. Use only suffixes which begin with vowels.

cram	rush	ship
fuzz	sun	clean
wet	wait	fast

Have the children tell why each of the other words do not require a double consonant; then have them print those words with suffixes that you tell them to use.

You may want to go over the directions in the workbook with the children. A capable class should be able to do the lesson independently after the class introduction.

ANSWER KEY

Page 70 (top)
short vowel, one consonant

Page 70 (bottom)

1. f *o* am — foamy
2. wi *nd* — windy
3. — funny
4. flu *ff* — fluffy
5. — buggy
6. — sloppy
7. dr *e* am — dreamy
8. fro *st* — frosty

Page 71

9. r *a* in — rained
10. — hugged
11. me *nd* — mended
12. — mopped
13. mi *ss* — missed
14. — clipped
15. — rubbed
16. gr *o* an — groaned

17. *e* at — eating
18. chi *ll* — chilling
19. — padding
20. — winning
21. pr *a* y — praying
22. — sledding
23. — runner
24. gra *nd* — grander
25. f *e* ed — feeder
26. sti *ff* — stiffer
27. p *a* i *nt* — painter
28. bu *zz* — buzzer
29. — digger
30. — grabber
31. so *ft* — softest
32. — saddest
33. d *e* ep — deepest
34. — fattest

EXTRA ACTIVITY

Have the children list all the words they can find in their reading story that have suffixes.

LESSON 3
Dropping *e* to Add Suffixes

Dropping Silent *e*—*workbook, pages 72 and 73*

Do the first exercise together with the class or print these samples on the board.

bake   baker   baked   baking

Have the children identify and circle the suffixes. Then tell them to look at what is left of the words and ask them what is different from the root word at the beginning of the row.

Drill the rule by having it read several times, and read in unison. Say the rule and let the children fill in words when you pause.

ANSWER KEY

Page 72 (top and middle)

tam *ed* tam *ing* tam *er* tam *est*
fin *er* fin *est* fin *ed* fin *ing*
smok *y* smok *ing* smok *ed*

1. long
2. e
3. *(See above.)*
4. e

Page 72 (bottom)

1. stony	4. hazy
2. greasy	5. bony
3. rosy	6. shiny

Page 73

7. fading	10. smiling
8. voting	11. blazing
9. hoping	12. trading

13. named	16. striped
14. hiked	17. glazed
15. waved	18. sneezed
19. rider	22. scraper
20. later	23. glider
21. timer	24. cruder
25. lamest	28. closest
26. purest	29. cutest
27. ripest	30. stalest

EXTRA ACTIVITY

Have this list of words printed on the board for the children to print, adding the suffixes *ed* and *ing*.

tap	whip
tape	wipe
hop	mop
hope	mope

LESSON 4
Adding Suffixes With Consonant Beginnings

Consonant Suffixes—*workbook, pages 74 and 75*

Print on the board the list of suffixes given at the top of page 74. Call attention to the new suffix *ness* and let the children add it orally to words you say such as these:

glad	sad	round	wet
soft	cold	bright	kind

(The suffix *ish* is also new but will not be taught until a later lesson.)

Review the rules for doubling consonants and dropping final *e*. Emphasize the part of the rule that states "a suffix that begins with a *vowel*." Have the children pick out the suffixes on the board that begin with consonants.

Demonstrate with the word *glad*. Have someone print the word on the board with a vowel suffix; then have someone print it with the suffix *ly*.

Use the word *like* for another sample. Have someone print the word with *ing*, and then with *ness* or *ly*.

Drill the rule given at the top of page 74.

ANSWER KEY

Page 74

1. hopeless	hopeful
2. restless	restful
3. joyless	joyful
4. doubtless	doubtful
5. harmless	harmful
6. careless	careful
7. faithless	faithful
8. painless	painful
9. cheerless	cheerful
10. fearless	fearful

Page 75 (top and middle)

11. lonely	14. widely
12. surely	15. likely
13. purely	16. lovely
17. kindness	21. ripeness
18. fitness	22. likeness
19. cuteness	23. wideness
20. drabness	24. redness

Page 75 (bottom)

1. short, one, double, vowel
2. e, drop, vowel
3. consonant

LESSON 5
Review

Suffix Rules—*workbook, pages 76 and 77*

Review the rules. Review the applications by practicing samples of each type on the board or by beginning the lesson as a class activity.

ANSWER KEY

Page 76

1. canner		7. dimmest	
2. resting	b	8. cupful	c
3. hatless	c	9. twister	b
4. soapy	a	10. tugged	
5. meanest	a	11. gladness	c
6. swimming		12. nutty	

Page 77

1. baker	16. slowly
2. sailing	17. stamped
3. hottest	18. hateful
4. sinner	19. waving
5. moaned	20. sandy
6. neatest	21. rotting
7. sunny	22. lateness
8. roaster	23. poked
9. widest	24. thinnest
10. duster	25. fretful
11. letting	26. drifting
12. boneless	27. rainy
13. oldest	28. nosy
14. spinner	29. hopped
15. longest	30. hoped

Gradebook: 30 points for page 77

EXTRA ACTIVITIES

1. Have the children print the number of syllables for each word after they have added the suffixes.

2. Tell the children to take the words between certain given numbers and try to print the root word with a different suffix.

LESSON 6
Changing *y* to Add Suffixes

Changing *y* to *i*—*workbook, pages 78 and 79***

Have the children do number one in the workbook or circle the suffixes in samples you have printed on the board. Then compare the remainder of the words with the original root word. State and drill the rule. Note that the change is made for suffixes beginning with consonants as well as for those beginning with vowels.

ANSWER KEY

Page 78 (top and middle)

cri *ed*   cri *es*   cri *er*

busi *er* busi *est* busi *ness*
    busi *ly*

happi *ness* happi *ly* happi *er*
    happi *est*

1.
2. yes
3. yes
4. y
5. consonant
6. It was changed to *i*.

Page 78 (bottom)

1. tries	tried
2. carries	carried
3. hurries	hurried
4. copies	copied

Page 79 (top)

5. drier	driest
6. sorrier	sorriest
7. cozier	coziest
8. chubbier	chubbiest

Page 79 (bottom)

9. fried	1	15. plentiful	3
10. pitied	2	16. merciless	3
11. pitiful	3	17. lazily	3
12. penniless	3	18. laziness	3
13. stories	2	19. beautiful	3
14. fuzziness	3	20. sloppily	3

LESSON 7
Changing *y* to Add Suffixes

Changing *y* to *i*—*workbook, pages 80 and 81***

Review the rules. Print *hurry* on the board and let someone print the word with the suffix *ed*. Then suggest adding the suffix *ing*. Let the children say what the word will be. Demonstrate what happens if you change the *y* to *i* before adding *ing*. You have two *i's* next to each other. To avoid that, we do not change the *y* when we are adding a suffix that begins with *i*.

Turn to page 80 in the workbook and ask the children to find another suffix that begins with *i*. Let them practice adding *ish* to words orally as you say this words: *small, child, fool, girl, sweet, gray, old, green.*

ANSWER KEY

Page 80 (top and middle)

carry *ing*   gray *ish*
boy *ish*   pity *ing*
play *ing*   baby *ish*
    copy *ing*   hurry *ing*
    bury *ing*   clay *ish*
    enjoy *ing*   obey *ing*

1.
2. y
3. b. Sometimes it is a consonant and sometimes a vowel.
4. i

Page 80 (bottom)

1.
2. fry   frying
3. dry   drying
4. carry   carrying
5. marry   marrying
6. try   trying
7. ready   readying

8. envy   envying
9. busy   busying

Page 81 (top)
1. consonant, i
2. begins, i

Page 81 (bottom)
1. flying	2
2. prayed	3
3. ponies	1
4. worrying	2
5. trays	3
6. handier	1
7. joyful	3
8. crying	2
9. grayest	3
10. cheerily	1
11. playful	3
12. heaviness	1
13. boyish	2 / 3

LESSON 8
Finding Root Words

A. Reversing Suffix Changes—*workbook, page 82*

Review the rules. For each rule, give a sample of a word with a suffix and let the children take the word apart and correctly spell the root word and the suffix separately.

B. Word Forms—*workbook, page 83*

Suggest root words and let the children think of as many forms of the word as they can by adding various suffixes. The children will need to choose their answers on the basis of their familiarity with word usage rather than by a rule taught in class.

ANSWER KEY

Page 82

1. joy   ful
2. happy   ness
3. drive   er
4. bake   ed
5. sand   y
6. red   ish
7. life   less
8. child   ish
9. fade   ing
10. story   es
11. obey   ing
12. lazy   est
13. cut   ing
14. nice   est
15. win   er
16. busy   ly

Page 83

1. busiest   busy
2. payment   pay
3. blacken   black
4. hopeless   hope
5. fooled   fool
6. weakest   weak
7. enjoyed   enjoy
8. gladness   glad

EXTRA ACTIVITY

Give a series of words formed from the same root word and let the children print a sentence for each form. Example: cheer—cheery, cheered, cheering, cheerful, cheerless

LESSON 9
Adding Prefixes

Prefixes—*workbook, pages 84 and 85*

Define the term *prefix* as "letters added at the beginning of words."

The children should be able to follow the directions on their own, but it may be well to discuss the meanings of some of the words.

ANSWER KEY

Page 84 (top)

a wake   *a* live   *a* round
a while   *a* sleep   *a* like
1. alike
2. awhile
3. asleep
4. awake
5. alive
6. around

Page 84 (bottom)

be came   *be* low   *be* long   *be* side
1. beside
2. became
3. below
4. belong

Page 85 (top)

de part   *de* lay   *de* light   *de* frost
1. depart
2. delight
3. delay
4. defrost

Page 85 (bottom)

re mind   *re* read   *re* print
re turn   *re* make   *re* tell
re write   *re* fill   *re* plant
1. remind
2. refill
3. replant
4. return
5. reread / retell

Gradebook: 42 points for the entire lesson

LESSON 10
Adding Prefixes

Prefixes—*workbook, pages 86 and 87*

Review the prefixes from Lesson 9. Introduce the ones used in Lesson 10 with samples for each one. Say some of the words from the list at the end of Lesson 10 and let the children tell you which prefix they recognize at the beginning of the word.

Teach the children to make careful lines that go between the letters and not on them.

ANSWER KEY

Page 86 (top)

fore finger   *fore* arm   *fore* head
fore noon   *fore* tell   *fore* fathers
1. forearm
2. forehead
3. forefinger
4. foretell
5. forenoon
6. forefathers

Page 86 (bottom)

dis obey   *dis* like   *dis* agree
dis trust   *dis* cover   *dis* please
1. displease
2. disobey
3. distrust
4. disagree
5. dislike
6. discover

Page 87 (top)

un fair   *un* lock   *un* tie
un wrap   *un* kind   *un* cover
un clean *un* done   *un* button

Page 87 (middle)
Individual sentences.

Page 87 (bottom)

1.
2. ex / tend
3. pre / fix
4. dis / appear
5. in / land
6. a / rise
7. re / pay
8. fore / sight
9. re / live
10. de / lay
11. be / little
12. un / happy
13. ex / plain
14. un / fold

15. be / neath
16. dis / color
17. fore / taste
18. de / scribe
19. in / come
20. pre / tend
21. a / head

EXTRA ACTIVITY

Have the children take the words from the top of page 87 and try to think of suffixes to add to them, printing words with both prefixes and suffixes.

LESSON 11
Prefixes and Suffixes

A. **Suffix Rules**—*workbook, page 88*
Review the rules, considering an example for each one.

B. **Recognizing Prefixes and Suffixes**—*workbook, page 89*
Self-explanatory.

ANSWER KEY

Page 88 (top)

1. short, one, vowel
2. drop, vowel
3. consonant
4. consonant, i
5. vowel
6. i

Page 88 (bottom)

6	2
3	5
1	4

Page 89

1.
2. twist / er   2
3. a / wake   2
4. re / store   2

5. a / lone / ness   3
6. pre / school   2
7. un / kind / est   3
8. de / tour   2
9. toast / y   2
10. in / vite   2
11. un / love / ly   3
12. dis / place   2
13. ex / pand / ed   3
14. seat / ed   2
15. fore / tell / ing 3
16. be / ware   2
17. tooth / less   2
18. cool / est   2
19. un / done   2
20. in / form / er   3
21. girl / ish   2

22. fly / ing	2
23. pre / tend / ed	3
24. ex / plode	2
25. re / cord / er	3
26. truth / ful	2
27. fore / cast	2
28. sure / ly	2

29. un / self / ish	3
30. firm / ness	2

Gradebook: 45 points for the entire lesson, counting only one point for correct division and syllable count on page 89

LESSON 12
Dividing Words Between Double Consonants

Double Consonants—*workbook, pages 90 and 91*

Tell the children that these words do not have prefixes and suffixes, but they have more than one syllable. "Words with more than one syllable have a proper place to divide them between the syllables, and we will be learning some of those rules."

ANSWER KEY

Page 90 (top)

let / ter	sum / mer	mit / ten
man / na	pil / low	bat / tle
bub / ble	kit / ten	bed / ding
les / son	pen / ny	car / rot
din / ner	fel / low	val / ley
lad / der	puz / zle	cab / bage
bot / tle	cat / tle	bug / gy
ar / row	rib / bon	ham / mer

Page 90 (bottom) *Answers may vary.*

Page 91 (top)

bet / ter	yel / low	hol / low
hap / py	rub / ber	jol / ly
fun / ny	stub / born	pret / ty
lit / tle	nar / row	rag / ged

Page 91 (second part) *Answers may vary.*

Page 91 (third part)

hap / pen	wad / dle	hur / ry
gal / lop	chat / ter	twit / ter
bor / row	car / ry	gob / ble

Page 91 (bottom) *Answers could vary.*

1. gallop	4. gobble
2. twitter	5. chatter
3. waddle	6. happen

EXTRA ACTIVITY

Lesson 12 in Unit 3 of the reader contains some words with spelling changes to add suffixes. See if the children can find words in which the consonant was doubled, words in which the *e* was dropped, and words in which the *y* was changed to *i*. Have them print the words and the root word for each one.

running	divided	hurried
winning	chasing	enemies
stopped	supposed	
	hiding	

LESSON 13
Dividing Words Between Two Consonants

A. Two Consonants—*workbook, page 92*

Review by printing samples on the board for the children to divide between prefixes, root words, and suffixes, and between double consonants. Introduce the new rule and give a few samples for practice.

B. Compound Words and Review—*workbook, page 93*

The last exercise on page 93 is a review of the different rules for division studied thus far.

ANSWER KEY

Page 92 (top)

gar / den	won / der	don / key
win / dow	gan / der	cap / tain
mas / ter	bur / den	fin / ger
win / ter	thun / der	trum / pet
bas / ket	blis / ter	bar / ley
sis / ter	mar / ket	fil / ter

Page 92 (bottom)

1. master, sister, captain
2. winter
3. window
4. garden
5. market
6. basket
7. gander / donkey
8. trumpet

Page 93 (top)

1. rain / bow
2. air / plane
3. wind / mill
4. mail / man
5. sun / set
6. cook / book
7. grape / vine
8. in / side
9. sun / shine
10. cob / web
11. rain / coat
12. tip / toe
13. life / boat
14. door / bell
15. home / work

Page 93 (bottom)

1. hus / band   2
2. but / ter   2
3. check / ing   2
4. yard / stick   2
5. dis / charge   2
6. com / ment   2
7. val / ley   2
8. up / stairs   2
9. pave / ment   2
10. fif / ty   2
11. moon / light   2
12. car / pet   2
13. pil / lar   2
14. re / port   2
15. cof / fee   2
16. some / where   2
17. green / ish   2
18. jour / ney   2
19. ex / claim   2
20. row / boat   2

EXTRA ACTIVITY

Have the children categorize words from page 93 (bottom). Under headings *compound words*, *words with prefixes*, and *words with suffixes*, have them print words they find in the lists.

LESSON 14
Review

A. Multiple Syllables—*workbook, page 94*

Suggest that the children first identify any prefix or suffix on each word and then consider the root word itself. Say the root word, listening for more than one syllable. In compound words, have them divide between the two words and then consider each part to see if it has more than one syllable.

B. Suffix Spelling Review—*workbook, page 95*

Review the rules for adding suffixes.

ANSWER KEY

Page 94

1.	un / hap / py	3
2.	gar / den / er	3
3.	win / dow / less	3
4.	fore / fin / ger	3
5.	day / dream / ing	3
6.	cold / est	2
7.	sis / ter / ly	3
8.	fore / noon	2
9.	de / part / ed	3
10.	bas / ket / ball	3
11.	dis / con / tent	3
12.	ex / change	2
13.	tea / spoon / ful	3
14.	pre / tend /er	3
15.	but / ter / fly	3
16.	sud / den / ly	3
17.	a / light	2
18.	home / sick / ness	3
19.	un / der / line	3
20.	bas / ket / ful	3
21.	be / lit / tle	3
22.	cot / ton / y	3
23.	but / ton / hole	3
24.	re / form	2
25.	un / bur / den	3
26.	boy / ish	2
27.	fel / low / ship	3
28.	in / vent / ed	3

Page 95

1. sagged
2. hardly
3. sinless
4. penniless
5. stony
6. plainest
7. fuzziness
8. thinking
9. riper
10. hopeful
11. thinnest
12. babyish
13. cleaning
14. cheery
15. cozily

Gradebook: 15 points for page 95

EXTRA ACTIVITY

Have the children print on a separate paper the root words they find in the list on page 94.

LESSON 15
Dividing Words With *le* Endings

Introducing the Rule—*workbook, pages 96 and 97*
State the rule and look at some of the words in the exercise. Point out that this rule agrees with the ones they learned about dividing between consonants.

ANSWER KEY

Page 96 (top)

1. cat / tle	11. pur / ple
2. pad / dle	12. jum / ble
3. tum / ble	13. kin / dle
4. twin / kle	14. jun / gle
5. can / dle	15. an / kle
6. gig / gle	16. rid / dle
7. ap / ple	17. ket / tle
8. mid / dle	18. tan / gle
9. sprin / kle	19. wig / gle
10. sim / ple	20. spar / kle

21. rip / ple
22. grum / ble
23. bun / dle
24. lit / tle
25. peb / ble
26. dim / ple
27. gen / tle
28. sin / gle
29. pud / dle
30. thim / ble

Page 96 (bottom)
1. tle, dle, ble, kle, gle, ple
2. 12
3. 18

Page 97
1. middle
2. puddle
3. pebble
4. ripple
5. ankle
6. grumble
7. little
8. tumble
9. purple
10. bundle
11. wiggle
12. giggle
13. tangle

EXTRA ACTIVITY
"Draw a picture for the sentences on page 97."

LESSON 16
Dividing Words With *ckle*

Words with *ckle*—*workbook, pages 98 and 99*
Review the rules studied so far for dividing syllables. Print *chuckle* on the board, and ask the children where that word might be divided according to the rules they have studied. Then ask them what two consonants they see in the middle of the word. Remind them that *ck* is a digraph, and tell them that we must not divide two letters that make one sound. In these words *ck* must stay with the first syllable, and the last syllable will be just two letters.

Print a selection of words on the board from the list at the top of page 99 to give the children practice in recognizing the *ck* words and remembering to divide them after the *k*.

ANSWER KEY

Page 98 (top and middle)

bu *ck* / le   cra *ck* / le   tri *ck* / le
ti *ck* / le   pi *ck* / le   spe *ck* / le
fre *ck* / le   chu *ck* / le   ca *ck* / le

1. yes
2. kle
3. c

Page 98 (bottom)

1. cackle
2. trickle
3. pickle
4. buckle
5. freckle
6. chuckle
7. tickle

Page 99 (top)

1. thim / ble   7. twin / kle
2. trick / le   8. buck / le
3. wrin / kle   9. an / kle
4. sick / le   10. speck / le
5. strug / gle   11. freck / le
6. han / dle   12. ruf / fle
            13. tur / tle
            14. crum / ple
            15. spar / kle
            16. shack / le
            17. driz / zle
            18. chuck / le

Page 99 (bottom) *These are possible sentences.*
Fido barked and barked at the turtle.
We will try to glue the broken handle.

LESSON 17
Accented Syllables

A. Identifying Accent—*workbook, page 100*

Have the children practice orally in class, saying the words in the list with exaggerated accent. Note that the *le* syllable is not accented. Note that prefixes and suffixes are not accented. State that as a general rule.

Have the children say the words in the exercise at the bottom of page 100 to see if they can pronounce the words as they are shown. If they have trouble shifting the accent from the accustomed syllable, show them how by pronouncing the words for them as they mark the word that sounds right in each set.

B. Dividing Syllables Review—*workbook, page 101*

Review the rules for dividing syllables. Tell the children that words sometimes need to be divided because the line on which one is printing becomes full before the whole word can be written. In such a case, the word must be divided at the correct place and a hyphen placed at the end of the line to show that the word is finished on the next line.

ANSWER KEY

Page 100 (bottom)
1. **think·**er
2.   be·**side**
3. **gray·**ish
4. **gob·**ble
5.   un·**fold**
6.   pre·**pare**
7. **can·**dle
8.   de·**stroy**
9. **fear·**less
10. **cloud·**y

Page 101 (top)
1. be / tween
2. hard / est
3. prob / lem
4. for / get
5. a / wake
6. clat / ter
7. sim / ple
8. may / be
9. re / mark
10. free / ly
11. in / dex
12. mar / ket
13. kit / ten
14. joy / ful
15. al / low
16. de / lay
17. bub / ble
18. six / ty

Page 101 (bottom)
1.
2. joy-ful
3. mar-ket
4. six-ty
5. for-get
6. a-wake

EXTRA ACTIVITIES
1. Have the children circle the accented syllable in each word in the lists at the top of page 101, going by the general rule of not accenting affixes or *le* syllables.

2. Have the children page through library books, skimming the right margin for hyphens. Have them print the divided words they find on a paper, showing the break between the syllables. Perhaps they will be able to show other breaks in words with multiple syllables.

LESSON 18
The Accent Mark

The Accent Mark—*workbook, pages 102 and 103*

Explain that the accent mark after a syllable means that whole syllable is to be said with more stress, just as the bold print letters indicate. Have them practice saying the words given for comparison of the bold print and the accent mark. Let them also practice saying the words in the exercise at the bottom of page 102. Can they say the words as the accents are shown? The exercise can be done simply by comparing the words and does not require ability to sound accents.

Ask the children what kind of syllables are generally not accented. (prefixes, suffixes, and *le* syllables)

Teach the children how to make the accent mark.

ANSWER KEY

Page 102
1. cov'·er
   be·hind'
3. la'·zy
4. ser'·vant
5. tem'·ple
6. wor'·ship
7.   be·low'
8.   a·gainst'
9. val'·ley
10.   pro·tect'
11. fam'·i·ly
12.   dis·ap·pear'
13.   ex·cite'·ment
14.   un·fold'·ing

Page 103 (top)
1. to·day'   7. hap'·pen
2. sec'·ond   8. com·mand'
3. re·ward'   9. hun'·dred
4. de·cide'   10. con·trol'
5. in·stead' 11. king'·dom
6. care'·ful 12. lead'·er

Page 103 (bottom)
1. careful
2. happen, second
3. leader, kingdom
4. instead
5. control (*or* command)
6. decide, today

LESSON 19
Accented Syllables

A. Pronunciation Symbols—*workbook, page 104*
The children will need to choose the correct pronunciation by sounding the letter symbols. They can place the accent mark by looking at the word given.

B. Dividing and Accenting—*workbook, page 105*
Tell the children that they need not use special pronunciation symbols in printing the words as was done on page 104. Have them simply print the word in separate syllables and mark the accented syllable. Review the types of syllables that are usually unaccented. If necessary, pronounce the words for the children to identify the accented syllable.

ANSWER KEY

Page 104

1.	X	(nar'·ō)	9.	X	(nā'·shun)
2.	X	(sėr'·tin)	10.	X	(a·mount')
3.	(tōō·nīt')	X	11.	(dag'·er)	X
4.	(kėr'·ij)	X	12.	(rē·mānd')	X
5.	X	(rē·mīnd')	13.	X	(i·maj'·in)
6.	(dē·zėrv')	X	14.	(sep'·a·rāt)	X
7.	(mes'·ij)	X	15.	X	(a·kôrd'·ing)
8.	X	(är'·mē)			

Page 105 (top)

1.
2. un / load   un·load'
3. mid / dle   mid'·dle
4. be / friend   be·friend'
5. pay / ment   pay'·ment
6. driz / zle   driz'·zle

7. re / prove   re·prove'
8. clear / ly   clear'·ly
9. sick / le   sick'·le
10. storm / y   storm'·y
11. crack / le   crack'·le
12. in / vent   in·vent'

Page 105 (bottom)

1. invent
2. befriend
3. drizzle
4. gentle
5. reprove
6. stormy
7. middle
8. unload

Gradebook: 46 points for the entire lesson

LESSON 20
Review

A. **Suffix Spellings**—*workbook, page 106 (top)*
Review the rules for adding suffixes.

B. **The Accent Mark**—*workbook, page 106 (bottom)*
For the short exercise on accents at the bottom of the page, review the rule that prefixes, suffixes, and *le* syllables are usually unaccented.

C. **Dividing Syllables**—*workbook, page 107*
Review the rules for dividing syllables.
Make it clear that the samples following each rule are *not* answers to be filled in the blanks.

ANSWER KEY

Page 106 (top)

1. fresher   freshest   freshness
2. gladder   gladdest   gladly
3. deeper   deepest   deeply
4. shines   shining   shiny
5. copier   copied   copying
6. sprayer   spraying   sprayed
7. careless   careful   caring

Page 106 (bottom)

1. firm'·ly   4. rid'·dle
2. un·wise'   5. re·lax'
3. new'·est   6. en·joy'

Page 107

1. root words
   un / seen   thought / ful
   in / tend / ed   be / long / ing
2. small
   mail / box   him / self
   with / out   fire / man
3. consonant, between
   but / ter   mil / lion   hap / pen
   nar / row
4. divide, consonants
   trum / pet   wan / der
   mon / key   lan / tern

5. three
   an / kle   mar / ble   bun / dle
   star / tle

6. ck
   tick / le   freck / le   cack / le
   buck / le

LESSON 21
The Schwa

Introducing the Symbol—*workbook, pages 108 and 109*

Print the schwa symbol on the board and tell the children what it is called. Tell the children that it is not a letter, but is used for other letters in a pronunciation especially when the sound is not said clearly enough to hear what the letter is. The schwa sound itself can best be described as a grunt with the mouth hanging open.

Let the children answer the questions on their own; then clarify the concepts that the schwa can represent any of the vowels and that it always appears in an unaccented syllable.

Teach the children to begin the schwa symbol with a clockwise curve as though they were making the round part of the letter *b*.

ANSWER KEY

Page 108 and 109

1. a. first
   b. second
   c. a
2. a. first
   b. second
   c. e
3. a. first
   b. second
   c. i
4. a. first
   b. second
   c. o

5. a. first
   b. second
   c. u
6. a. second
   b. first
   c. a
7. a. second
   b. first
   c. e
8. a, e, i, o, u

LESSON 22
The Schwa

A. As a Modified Vowel—*workbook, page 110*

The pronunciation formerly shown as *ėr* may be printed with the schwa symbol if it is not in an accented syllable. Point out the difference between the two syllables in the pronunciation of *murmur*, and the relation of the accent.

B. In the *le* Syllables—*workbook, page 111*

The pronunciations formerly shown as *ʹl* may be printed with the schwa symbol. It is convenient to avoid the apostrophe as a vowel symbol from this point on to prevent confusion with the accent mark.

Remembering the rule that the schwa is used only in unaccented syllables, the children can place the accent marks in the exercise by looking at the word.

ANSWER KEY

Page 110

1. neighb *o* r
2. begg *a* r
3. s *u* rprise
4. anch *o* r
5. ced *a* r
6. h *u* rrah
7. f *e* rment
8. c *o* rrect
9. cell *a* r
10. h *e* rself
11. farm *e* r
12. coll *a* r
13. p *u* rsue
14. s *u* rvive
15. col *o* r
16. p *e* rform

Page 111

<u>e</u> 1. (bob'·ən)
<u>i</u> 2. (sėr'·kəl)
<u>f</u> 3. (skwėr'·əl)
<u>a</u> 4. (kuz'·ən)
<u>j</u> 5. (sə·round')
<u>g</u> 6. (ə·dôrn')
<u>b</u> 7. (jung'·gəl)
<u>c</u> 8. (ə·līv')
<u>h</u> 9. (sel'·dəm)
<u>k</u> 10. (hab'·ət)
<u>d</u> 11. (sər·mīz')

LESSON 23
Vowel Symbols

A. Printing Vowel Symbols—*workbook, page 112*

Remind the children that the schwa symbol is used only in unaccented syllables. That rule will automatically tell them where to use the schwa symbol in the exercise. The other vowel symbol will have to be printed by hearing the sound. (Here as in other lessons, /o/ may be use for /ô/.)

B. Printing Sentences—*workbook, page 113*

Suggest that the children look over the word lists on page 112 for some possible words to use in their sentences. Do not hinder their originality, however, by requiring them to use words from the list.

ANSWER KEY

Page 112

1. ā ə	7. ô ə	13. ē ə	20. ē ə
2. ə ä	8. i ə	14. ī ə	21. ė ə
3. e ə	9. ə e	15. ə e	22. a ə
4. ô ə	10. ə ä	16. ē ə	23. ə ė
5. ə e	11. ė ə	17. ə ō	24 o͞o ə
6. u ə	12. ū ə	18. ā ə	25. ė ə
		19. ə ā	26. ė ə

Page 113 *These are possible sentences.*

1. It was very peaceful at the cabin.
2. All the pupils enjoyed that lesson.
3. Did the people blame the driver?

Gradebook: 55 points for the entire lesson

EXTRA ACTIVITY

Let the children print a story of several sentences or paragraphs for one of the pictures on page 113.

LESSON 24
The Breve

A. The Breve—*workbook, page 114*

Introduce the breve as a mark for a vowel with the short sound just like the unmarked vowels they have studied. Teach the children to make neat, small breve that covers just one letter.

B. Printing Pronunciations—*workbook, page 115*

Print some samples on the board and have the children practice each step of the directions. Caution the children to consider the consonant sounds as they print the pronunciations. The letters *ck* should be represented by *k*. Sometimes *s* should be represented by *z*. Also have the children place the accent mark before the dot when the first syllable is accented.

ANSWER KEY

Page 114

1. cr ă sh
2. l ī ght
3. sh ĭ p
4. m ŭ ch
5. sh ä rp
6. t ē ach
7. h ė r
8. str ĕ ngth
9. str ô ng
10. c ō ast
11. scr ā pe
12. wh ĭ ch
13. s ô ft
14. m ū le
15. th ă nk
16. spl ŏ tch
17. m ā in
18. cl ă p
19. c ū te
20. sn ĭ ff

21. cl ė rk
22. b ĕ st
23. sp ē ed
24. f ä rm
25. w ī pe
26. cr ŏ ps
27. f ė rn
28. scr ŭ b
29. fr ĕ sh
30. fr ō ze

Page 115

1.
2. rock / er (rŏk'·ər)
3. a / live (ə·līv')
4. mend / ed (mĕnd'·əd)
5. dish / es (dĭsh'·əz)
6. a / sleep (ə·slēp')
7. trust / ed (trŭst'·əd)
8. dark / est (därk'·əst)
9. dis / please (dĭs·plēz')
10. burn / ing (bėrn'·ĭng)
11. in / deed (ĭn·dēd')
12. rain / ing (rān'·ĭng)
13. un / rest (ŭn·rĕst')
14. kind / ness (kīnd'·nĕs)
15. law / less (lô'·lĕs)
16. un / true (ŭn·trōō')

LESSON 25
Review of Vowel Symbols

A. The Breve for *oo*—*workbook, page 116*
   Teach the children to draw the breve to cover the two *o*'s in the digraph.
   Tell them that /ä/ and /ŏ/ represent the same sound. The /ä/ symbol is usually used when this sound is spelled with the letter *a*.

B. Vowel Symbol Review—*workbook, page 117*
   Self-explanatory

ANSWER KEY

Page 116

1. c o͞o l,   t o͝o k,   w o͝o ds
2. m o͞o n,   r o͞o f
3. st o͝o d,   l o͝o k,   g o͞o d
4. S o͞o n,   m o͞o n,   p o͞o l
5. l o͝o ked,   bl o͞o m
6. br o͝o k,   m o͞o n,   t o͞o
7. sh o͝o k
8. f o͝o t
9. l o͝o ked,   b o͝o k,   m o͞o n

Page 117 (top)

1. sunny ——— ā
2. they ——— ē
3. fly ——————— ī
4. few ——— ō
5. show ——— ū

6. bubble ——— ă
7. flatly ——— ĕ
8. bread ——— ĭ
9. tricky ——— ŏ
10. gobble ——— ŭ

11. swat ——————— ä
12. thoughtless ——— ė
13. could ——— ə
14. firmly ——— ô
15. awake ——— o͞o

16. grew ——— ō
17. push ——— ŏ
18. caught ——— ô
19. though ——— o͞o
20. stopping ——— o͝o

Page 117 (bottom)

1. d	5. g
2. b	6. e
3. a	7. f
4. c	8. h

Gradebook: 28 points for page 117

EXTRA ACTIVITY
   Give a capable student access to a science book or other reference book in which he can gather some information about the moon.

LESSON 26
Review of Adding Suffixes

Review—*workbook, pages 118 and 119*
   You may want to review the rules again in class drill. It may help to prevent confusion on page 119 if you have the children first circle the suffixes and underline the root words. They may be able to associate the rules more easily with the parts marked.

ANSWER KEY

Page 118

1. double, vowel
   circled words: beg, flap, knot, trip, club
2. drop, vowel
   underlined words: hide, wave, use, paste, chime, joke
3. y, i
   boxed words: dry, tasty, hasty, happy, busy
4. i

Page 119

1.	~~thinnly~~	thinly
2.	~~taping~~	tapping
3.	~~rustty~~	rusty
4.	~~skateing~~	skating
5.	~~timless~~	timeless
6.	~~hopful~~	hopeful
7.	~~whitness~~	whiteness
8.	~~deepper~~	deeper
9.	~~flyes~~	flies
10.	~~plaiful~~	playful
11.	~~fuzzyer~~	fuzzier
12.	~~enjoiment~~	enjoyment

EXTRA ACTIVITY

Have the children alphabetize each of the first two sets of words on page 118.

LESSON 27
Review of Syllabication

Review—*workbook, pages 120 and 121*

Conduct class review on the rules for dividing syllables. Point out that the *le* words could also fit in the double-consonant or two-consonant sections, but they should not be used there.

ANSWER KEY

1. a / stray
   re / store
   de / light

2. fear / less
   teach / ing
   soft / ly

3. a / lone / ness
   un / like /ly

4. birth / day
   day / dream

5. gen / tle
   tan / gle
   crum / ple
   pick / le

un / told
fore / head
be / side

round / ness
dish / es
use / ful

re / pair / ing
dis / taste / ful

rain / bow
fire / light

mar / ble
buck / le
han / dle
driz / zle

6. sup / per
   ham / mer
   kit / ten

7. ras / cal
   gar / lic
   bas / ket

fol / low
rab / bit
muf / fin

num /ber
win / dow
af / ter

EXTRA ACTIVITY

Alphabetize any or all of the sections of words after they have been placed into the right category according to division of syllables.

LESSON 28
Review of Pronunciation Symbols

A. Vowel Symbols—*workbook, page 122*
Self-explanatory.

B. Vowel Symbols and Accents—*workbook, page 123 (top)*
Remind the children to watch for prefixes, suffixes, and *le* to help them determine which syllable is accented. You may still need to pronounce the words for them to identify the accent in some words.

C. Word Pronunciation—*workbook, page 123 (bottom)*
Self-explanatory.

ANSWER KEY

Page 122
1. higher   ā
2. field ———— ē
3. neighbor   ī
4. open ———— ō
5. mule ———— ū

6. ready   ă
7. gobble   ĕ
8. cabin   ĭ
9. husky   ŏ
10. shiver   ŭ

11. purpose   ä
12. partake   ė
13. pushing   ô
14. pause   ə
15. pursue   o͞o

16. stove ———— ō
17. scoop   ŏ
18. straw   ô
19. stop   o͞o
20. should ———— o͝o

21. plank   ā
22. play   ă
23. park ———— ä
24. asleep   ô
25. paws   ə

26. perching   ē
27. higher   ĕ
28. obey   ė
29. donkey   ə
30. headlight   ā

Page 123 (top)
1. (thŭn'·dər)   8. (ə·hĕd')
2. (əb·tān')   9. (səb·mĭt')
3. (kūt'·əst)   10. (măt'·ər)
4. (pə·līt')   11. (sē'·zən)
5. (ə·gō')   12. (tėr'·nəp)
6. (mär'·tən)   13. (ho͝od'·əd)
7. (fŏks'·əz)   14. (ə·loud')

Page 123 (bottom)
1. (pärt'·lē)   7. (plăs'·tĭk)
2. (ŭp·hōld')   8. (ŭn·jŭst')
3. (fôl'·ĭng)   9. (po͞od'·ĭng)
4. (pŏp'·ē)   10. (trăf·ĭk)
5. (wėr'·shĭp)   11. (ŭn·tī')
6. (dĭs·tėrb')   12. (ŭn·răp')

EXTRA ACTIVITY
Alphabetize the words in the first two groups of the matching exercise on page 123.

LESSON 29
Review

Review—*workbook, pages 124 and 125*
The words in this lesson all use the schwa in the unaccented syllables and only long or short vowels in the other syllables.

ANSWER KEY

Pages 124 and 125 *Part c for each number is individual work.*

1. a. un / der   b. (ŭn'·dər)
2. a. pen / cil   b. (pĕn'·səl)
3. a. po / lite   b. (pə·līt')
4. a. pat / tern   b. (păt'·ərn)
5. a. a / lone   b. (ə·lōn')
6. a. scat / ter   b. (skăt'ər)
7. a. a / sleep   b. (ə·slēp')
8. a. prob / lem   b. (prŏb'·ləm)

LESSON 30
Review

Review—*workbook, pages 126 and 127*
These words do not use the schwa sound, but they do include the modified vowel sounds /ä/, /ô/, and /ė/.

ANSWER KEY

Pages 126 and 127 *Part c for each number is individual work.*

1. a. farm / ing   b. (färm'·ĭng)
2. a. thirst / y   b. (thėrst'·ē)
3. a. short / ly   b. (shôrt'·lē)
4. a. un / cooked   b. (ŭn·ko͝okt')
5. a. en / joy   b. (ĕn·joi')
6. a. count / ing   b. (kount'·ĭng)
7. a. tru / ly   b. (tro͞o'·lē)
8. a. in / vite   b. (ĭn·vīt')

TEST

ANSWER KEY

A.
1. wetter
2. sagging
3. muddy
4. gladly
5. rained
6. shortness
7. baker
8. ripest
9. smiling
10. careful
11. lovely
12. hurried
13. plentiful
14. prayed
15. trying

B. *The prefixes in bold print should be circled, and the suffixes should be underlined.*
1. **fore** noon
2. **a** like
3. laugh ing
4. **be** side
5. fish ed
6. **de** lay
7. brush es
8. cold er
9. **dis** please
10. wild est
11. harm less
12. rock y
13. slow ly
14. **in** vent ed
15. **un** self ish
16. **pre** tend ing
17. **de** light ful
18. **a** lone ness
19. **un** kind ly
20. **re** fill s

C.
1. mit / ten
2. ar / row
3. cap / tain
4. sis / ter
5. cook / book
6. home / work
7. fast / est
8. dis / like
9. pur / ple
10. tick / le
11. han / dle
12. freck / le
13. bas / ket / ball
14. sud / den / ly
15. dis / trust / ful
16. un / end / ing

D.
1. (dĭs·mā')   5. (nē'dəl)
2. (ŭn·trōō')   6. (sə·pōz')
3. (kīnd'nĕss)   7. (ə·wā')
4. (rān'ĭng)   8. (pĕn'·səl)

E.
1. (băk)   6. (shėrt)
2. (härt)   7. (bēz)
3. (tėrn)   8. (wĕl)
4. (chĭn)   9. (fū)
5. (krŏps)   10. (thôrn)

Gradebook: 100 test points, counting one for each affix in part B, one for each division in part C, and three for each pronunciation in part E.

Unit 4

UNIT 4
General Plan

Unit 4 reviews a few consonant digraphs and introduces some new syllabication rules. Practice is given with contractions and homophones.

Remove and file the tests for Units 4 and 5 before distributing the workbooks.

Phonics Lessons Unit 4

LESSON 1
The Digraph *gh*

Phonics Class—*workbook, pages 6 and 7*

Review the definition and samples of digraphs, and teach *gh* as a digraph that says /f/. Let the children read the sentences orally. If they cannot read the *gh* words, have them do the top part on page 7 and study the sentences, and then read orally later, perhaps when you check the lesson.

The word meanings for the bottom part on page 7 should be gathered by considering the context in the sentences on page 6.

ANSWER KEY

Page 6 (top)

A digraph is *two* letters together that make *one* sound.

sh oe *th* in wi *ng* *sh* arp
pa *ck* pea *ch* mo *th* er *wh* y
pa *th* *th* ey *wh* eel stu *ng*

Page 6 (bottom)

1. enou *gh*
2. cou *gh* ing
3. rou *gh*
4. lau *gh*
5. trou *gh*
6. tou *gh*
7. rou *gh* ly
8. lau *gh* ter
9. cou *gh*
10. tou *gh* en

Page 7 (top)

1. laugh
2. tough
3. coughing
4. trough
5. enough
6. toughen
7. laughter

Page 7 (bottom)

1. cough / coughing
2. rough
3. enough
4. laughter / laugh
5. trough
6. toughen
7. roughly

EXTRA ACTIVITY

Have the children find other consonant digraphs in the sentences on page 6 and put a color spot on each one.

LESSON 2
The Digraph *ph*

Phonics Class—*workbook, pages 8 and 9*

Review *gh* and teach *ph* as a digraph. Have the children read the sentences orally, allowing time for study of the pronunciations first if necessary.

As in Lesson 1, the children should be able to understand the word meanings from the context.

ANSWER KEY

Page 8

1. tele *ph* one
2. ne *ph* ew
3. *ph* otogra *ph*
4. trium *ph*, *Ph* araoh
5. *ph* rase
6. digra *ph*
7. di *ph* thong
8. *ph* easant
9. ele *ph* ant
10. gra *ph*
11. pam *ph* let
12. paragra *p*h
13. al *ph* abet

Page 9 (top)
1. nephew
2. graph

3. digraph
4. triumph
5. pamphlet
6. diphthong
7. photograph

Page 9 (bottom)
1. paragraph
2. pheasant
3. elephant
4. photograph
5. alphabet
6. telephone
7. triumph
8. phrase
9. Pharaoh

Gradebook: 31 points for the entire lesson

LESSON 3
The Sound /zh/

Phonics Class—*workbook, pages 10 and 11*

Teach the children to recognize and say the /zh/ sound. It is formed in the same way as /sh/ but carries a voiced buzz with it. Have them practice saying the words on page 10.

Let the children compare the words in previous lessons to find the correct digraph for page 11 (top).

ANSWER KEY

Page 10 (top)
1. clo *s* ure
2. lei *s* ure
3. sei *z* ure
4. mea *s* ure
5. trea *s* ure
6. plea *s* ure
7. a *z* ure
8. vi *s* ion

Page 10 (bottom)
1. measure
2. leisure
3. pleasure
4. azure
5. treasure
6. vision

Page 11 (top)

1. lau *gh*
2. di *ph* thong
3. pam *ph* let
4. *ph* otogra *ph*
5. cou *gh*
6. paragra *ph*
7. ne *ph* ew
8. rou *gh* ly
9. gra *ph*
10. *ph* rase
11. rou *gh*
12. lau *gh* ter
13. tou *gh* en
14. tele *ph* one
15. ele *ph* ant
16. tou *gh* est
17. trou *gh*
18. *Ph* araoh
19. enou *gh*
20. cou *gh* ing
21. *ph* easant
22. tou *gh*
23. trium *ph*
24. digra *ph*

Page 11 (bottom)
Individual work.

EXTRA ACTIVITY

Have the children alphabetize the words given on page 10 (top).

LESSON 4
The Sound of *tion*

Phonics Class—*workbook, pages 12 and 13*

Print *tion* on the board. Tell the children that words that have this ending usually have the /sh/ sound for the *ti*. Underline the letters *ti*. Print *na* before the *tion* and let the children say the word. Then change the beginning to *sta, no, men, ac*, etc. Challenge the children to pronounce the list on page 12 and the words at the bottom of page 13. Discuss word meanings and let the children compose sentences for some of the words.

Words for the sentences on page 13 (top) are in the list on page 12.

ANSWER KEY

Page 12

1. na *tion*
2. lo *tion*
3. no *tion*
4. mo *tion*
5. sta *tion*
6. vaca *tion*
7. frac *tion*
8. men *tion*
9. cau *tion*
10. fic *tion*
11. addi *tion*
12. invita *tion*
13. founda *tion*
14. affec *tion*
15. educa *tion*

Page 13 (top)

1. nation
2. mention
3. motion
4. vacation
5. lotion
6. addition

Page 13 (bottom)

1. fic *tion*
2. fric *tion*
3. por *tion*
4. men *tion*
5. sta *tion*
6. sec *tion*
7. ac *tion*
8. trac *tion*
9. na *tion*
10. no *tion*
11. cau *tion*
12. lo *tion*
13. inven *tion*
14. instruc *tion*
15. destruc *tion*
16. popula *tion*
17. educa *tion*
18. invita *tion*

LESSON 5
The Sound of *ti, si, ci*

Phonics Class—*workbook, pages 14 and 15*

Print *mention* on the board and review the *tion* ending. Print *mansion* for comparison and tell the children that *si* also says /sh/. The letters *ci* also say /sh/, and the word endings are often other than *on*. Print various words for example and practice.

Review the distinction between /sh/ and /zh/. Let the children practice orally reading the words on page 15.

ANSWER KEY

Page 14

c	1. pre *ci* ous
e	2. vi *ci* ous
b	3. pa *ti* ent
f	4. pen *si* on
a	5. pa *ti* ence
g	6. an *ci* ent
d	7. par *ti* al
i	8. man *si* on
j	9. mo *ti* on
l	10. fa *ci* al
m	11. so *ci* al
h	12. expres *si* on
k	13. poten *ti* al
n	14. artifi *ci* al

Page 15 *Answers are interchangeable within sections.*

/f/	/zh/	/sh/
toughest	seizure	ancient
nephew	leisure	pension
orphan	measure	mansion
prophet	pleasure	precious
laugh	azure	patient
enough	usual	notion
alphabet	treasure	partial
trough	visual	mention

Gradebook: 52 points for the whole lesson

EXTRA ACTIVITY

Alphabetize the words in the /zh/ list. The /f/ list has only one duplicate of initial letters. The /sh/ list has several.

LESSON 6
Review of Syllabication

Phonics Class—*workbook, pages 16 and 17*

Review the syllabication rules.

ANSWER KEY

Pages 16 and 17 (top)

1. consonants

rab / bit	hap / py	bag / gage
les / son	muf / fin	sum / mer

2. two, consonants

en / ter	cap / tain
blan / ket	mar / tin
bas / ket	
lum / ber	

3. three

gur / gle	mar / ble
ket / tle	sam / ple
twin / kle	
can / dle	

4. ck

pick / le	trick / le
chuck / le	freck / le
buck / le	
tack / le	

5. root words

re / pay	slow / ly
be / side	good / ness
un / thank / ful	
in / tend / ing	

6. compound

fish / hook	sun / beam
bed / time	door / bell
day / light	
home / made	

Page 17 (bottom)

1. sis / ter	7. per / fect / ly
2. dark / ness	8. child / hood
3. chap / ter	9. hap / pen / ing
4. cir / cle	10. work / book
5. fur / nish	11. but / ter / fly
6. man / ner	12. un / paint / ed

13. birth / day
14. but / ton / hole
15. af / ter / noon
16. cor / rect / ness
17. re / turn / ing
18. a / bid / ing

LESSON 7
Syllabication Formula—v̄/cv

Phonics Class—*workbook, pages 18 and 19*

Do the first part of page 18 with the class or have them do it before class and rivet the rule by discussion. Print some samples on the board for the children to divide.

All the words on page 19 fit the new pattern. The rule can help the children do the words they do not know.

ANSWER KEY

Page 18 (top)

1. one
2. long
3. before
9. no / tion
10. no / tice
11. o / dor
12. to / ken

Page 18 (bottom)

1. va / por	5. mo / lar
2. pa / per	6. ma / son
3. ri / val	7. o / val
4. ra / ven	8. ti / ger

Page 19

1. mo / ment	mo
2. hu / man	hu
3. tri / pod	tri
4. fla / vor	fla

5. mo / tor	mo	17. su / per	su
6. u / nit	u	18. fe / ver	fe
7. o / ver	o	19. pre / vent	pre
8. la / bel	la	20. pro / nounce	pro
9. mo / tion	mo	21. spi / der	spi
10. vo / cal	vo	22. lo / cust	lo
11. sta / tion	sta	23. re / sult	re
12. to / tal	to	24. mi / nor	mi
13. i / ris	i	25. so / lo	so
14. slo / gan	slo	26. o / bey	o
15. pho / to	pho	27. so / cial	so
16. re / gion	re	28. ra / dar	ra

LESSON 8
Syllabication Formula—v̆c/v

Phonics Class—*workbook, pages 20 and 21*

Let the children do the first part of the lesson on their own; then discuss their findings in class. Review the rule from Lesson 7 and point out the difference. Print a pair of words such as *lima* and *limit* and observe the difference in pronunciation and syllabication.

All the words in the lesson follow the new short-vowel rule.

Discuss the bottom of page 21 after the children have done the lesson. Relate the rules for vowel sounds in one-syllable words to the first syllable of longer words. Compare the syllables the children printed for Lessons 7 and 8. Let the children read their lists of syllables.

ANSWER KEY

Page 20 (top)
1. one
2. short
3. after

Page 20 (bottom)

1. ped / al	5. sliv / er
2. hab / it	6. cab / in
3. reb / el	7. sec / ond
4. shov / el	8. tal / ent
9. prov / erb	
10. sev / en	
11. wag / on	
12. stud / y	

Page 21 (top)

1. sol / id	sol
2. trav / el	trav
3. rob / in	rob
4. pun / ish	pun
5. cred / it	cred
6. liz / ard	liz
7. rad / ish	rad
8. mod / el	mod
9. trem / or	trem
10. sol / emn	sol
11. com / et	com

12. prop / er   prop
13. sal / ad   sal
14. lil / y   lil
15. riv / er   riv
16. reb / el   reb
17. pan / el   pan
18. shek / el   shek
19. col / or   col
20. plan / et   plan
21. prov / erb   prov
22. at / om   at

Page 21 (bottom)

r ŏ b   p ă n   pr ŏ p   m ē
g ō   sh ē   s ō   m ĕ t

1. long
2. short

EXTRA ACTIVITY

Let the children take the syllables they printed for page 21 (top) and try adding other letters or syllables to make new words.
Examples: sol—solemn
trav—traverse
rob—Robert
pun—punch
You may let them use a dictionary to help.

LESSON 9
Review of Syllabication Formulas

Phonics Class—*workbook, pages 22 and 23*

Review the two rules from Lessons 7 and 8. Help the children realize that knowing the vowel sound tells them where to divide the word.

Although some of the words on page 23 (bottom) have more than one middle consonant, they may be divided by ending long vowel syllables with the vowel and short vowel syllables with one consonant. The resulting division should agree with the rule for words ending with *le*.

ANSWER KEY

1. rav / el	rav		15. prop / er	prop
2. ra / ven	ra		16. pro / pel	pro
3. so / lar	so		17. se / vere	se
4. sol / id	sol		18. sev / er	sev
5. riv / er	riv		19. res / in	res
6. ri / val	ri		20. re / sort	re
7. re / buke	re		21. se / nile	se
8. reb / el	reb		22. sen / ate	sen
9. ven / om	ven		23. rob / in	rob
10. Ve / nus	Ve		24. ro / bot	ro
11. rad / ish	rad		25. lil / y	lil
12. ra / dar	ra		26. li / lac	li
13. to / paz	to		27. sat / in	sat
14. top / ic	top		28. Sa / tan	Sa

Page 23 (top)

1. ī	7. ŭ	13. ĕ
2. ū	8. ō	14. ē
3. ĭ	9. ī	15. ō
4. ā	10. ō	16. ē
5. ă	11. ă	17. ĭ
6. ō	12. ā	18. ŏ

Page 23 (bottom)

1. tā / ble	7. bŭn / dle
2. jŭn / gle	8. stā / ble
3. ēa / gle	9. hăn / dle
4. nēe / dle	10. nōō / dles
5. bū / gle	11. rĭd / dle
6. thĭm / ble	12. crā / dle

13. bēe / tle
14. kĭn / dle
15. mā / ple
16. kĕt / tle
17. stēe / ple
18. tăn / gle

Gradebook: 64 points for the whole lesson

EXTRA ACTIVITY

The children should be able to pronounce by rule all the words in the lesson, but they will not likely know all the meanings. Have them print on paper a list of words that are unfamiliar; then hold a discussion period to explain some of the words and use them in sentences. If the children are able to find them in the dictionary, you may want to see what they can learn on their own.

LESSON 10
Syllabication With Medial Consonant Digraphs

Phonics Class—*workbook, pages 24 and 25*

Review the rules for dividing words with one consonant in the middle. Teach the idea of treating a consonant digraph as one letter.

ANSWER KEY

Page 24 (top)

1. b ā / by	10. t ī / ny	19. n ō / tice
2. s ĕ v / en	11. l ā / dy	20. ch ō / sen
3. c ă m / el	12. p ā / per	21. R ā / hab
4. ē / ven	13. n ĕ v / er	22. r ĕ f / uge
5. r ĭ v / er	14. c ī t / y	23. E / hud
6. ĕ v / er	15. p ō / ny	24. n ā / tion
7. ō / bey	16. d ū / ty	25. f ĭ g / ure
8. w ă g / on	17. d ĕ s / ert	26. r ā / zor
9. ĭ m / age	18. w ĭ d / ow	27. h ŏ n / or

Page 24 (bottom)
1. consonant, long
2. divide, first, short

Page 25 (top)

1. th	7. ck	13. sh
2. ck	8. ph	14. ph
3. ck	9. ch	15. sh
4. gh	10. th	16. gh
5. th	11. ph	17. ck
6. ph	12. sh	18. th

Page 25 (bottom)

1. rath / er	7. rock / er
2. pick / et	8. proph / et
3. duck / ling	9. rich / ly
4. laugh / ter	10. ei / ther
5. with / er	11. hy / phen
6. a / phid	12. wash / er

13. ash / es
14. as / phalt
15. sea / shell
16. tough / en
17. wick / ed
18. nei / ther

LESSON 11
Review

Phonics Class—*workbook, pages 26 and 27*
Review special sounds and their spellings.
Review rules for adding suffices by having the children practice samples on the board.

ANSWER KEY

Page 26

1. a	6. e
2. c	7. a
3. d	8. c
4. e	9. b
5. b	10. d
11. b	16. e
12. d	17. b
13. c	18. d
14. a	19. a
15. e	20. c
21. d	26. a
22. e	27. c
23. c	28. d
24. b	29. e
25. a	30. b

Page 27

1. canning	9. lovely
2. hottest	10. likeness
3. muddy	11. babies
4. restful	12. merrily
5. minded	13. grayness
6. baker	14. pitying
7. rising	15. boyish
8. changeless	

EXTRA ACTIVITY

Let the children take the root words given on page 27 and add various suffixes.

LESSON 12
Dividing Syllables Between Vowels

Phonics Class—*workbook, pages 28 and 29*

Have the children do page 28 (top) on their own; then rivet the rule in class discussion.

The words for the sentences on page 29 may be found at the top and bottom of page 28.

ANSWER KEY

Page 28 (top)
1. yes
2. no
3. no
4. yes
5. yes

Page 28 (bottom)
1. ri / ot
2. cru / el
3. gi / ant
4. Si / am
5. No / ah
6. qui / et
7. ne / on
8. di / et
9. flu / id
10. Le / on
11. po / et
12. li / on

Page 29
1. sci-ence
2. cru-el
3. cre-ate
4. gi-ant
5. li-on
6. po-em
7. No-ah
8. qui-et
9. fu-el

EXTRA ACTIVITY

Have the children draw a picture for one of the sentences on page 29.

LESSON 13
Review of Syllabication

Phonics Class—*workbook, pages 30 and 31*

Review the rules for dividing words with two consonants, one consonant, or two vowels.

ANSWER KEY

Page 30 (top)
1. man / ner
2. rib / bon
3. Peg / gy
4. mag / net
5. cor / ner
6. nap / kin
7. sim / ple
8. bub / ble
9. pa / per
10. co / coa
11. sev / en
12. la / bor
13. fin / ish
14. rob / in
15. la / dy
16. mo / tion
17. di / al
18. sci / ence
19. Le / on
20. gi / ant
21. ri / ot
22. cre / ate
23. po / em
24. no / el

Pages 30 (bottom) and 31
1. la-dy
2. di-al
3. rib-bon / pa-per
4. bub-ble
5. Peg-gy / Le-on
6. mag-net
7. fin-ish
8. po-em

9. cor-ner
10. sev-en
11. sci-ence
12. co-coa
13. gi-ant
14. nap-kin

Gradebook: 38 points for the whole lesson

LESSON 14
Contractions With *not*

Phonics Class—*workbook, pages 32 and 33*

Discuss the definition and samples at the beginning of the lesson. Have the children practice writing some contractions on the board. Point out the change in pronunciation of *do not* and the irregular spelling and pronunciation for *will not*.

Emphasize that the directions ask for a contraction in *each* sentence given on page 33. Review capital letters and periods as marks that indicate sentence beginnings and endings. You may wish to have students read the sentences one at a time and pick out and circle the words which will make the contractions.

ANSWER KEY

Page 32
1. aren't
2. couldn't
3. doesn't
4. hasn't
5. weren't
6. isn't
7. shouldn't
8. haven't
9. don't
10. didn't
11. hadn't
12. wouldn't
13. wasn't

Page 33

Judy said, "I ***don't*** know where Frank is. I ***can't*** find him in the house. He ***isn't*** with Father." Then she saw that his kites ***weren't*** in his room. "We ***won't*** wait for him," she decided.

EXTRA ACTIVITY

Have the children continue the story on page 33 using paper to finish it. Let them disregard the matter of contractions in their original writing.

LESSON 15
Other Contractions

Phonics Class—*workbook, pages 34 and 35*

Have the children identify the letters omitted in the sample contractions. Practice a few samples on the board, telling the children which letters to drop.

ANSWER KEY

Page 34

1. he'd	9. you're	11. a	16. d
2. I'd	10. they're	12. c	17. a
3. they'd	11. we're	13. e	18. b
4. he's	12. I'm	14. d	19. e
5. we've	13. she'll	15. b	20. c
6. you've	14. I'll		
7. he's	15. we'd	21. a	26. e
8. she's	16. she'd	22. c	27. d
		23. e	28. c

Page 35

		24. d	29. b
1. c	6. c	25. b	30. a
2. e	7. e		
3. d	8. d	**Gradebook:** 30 points for page 35	
4. a	9. a		
5. b	10. b		

LESSON 16
Using Contractions

Phonics Class—*workbook, pages 36 and 37*

Have the children orally respond with a contraction for two words that you say.

ANSWER KEY

Pages 36 and 37 *The sentence endings are individual work.*

1. I'd like to see . . .
2. You'll have to wait until . . .
3. He's often said . . .
4. She'd baked a . . .
5. We're ready to . . .
6. They've planted . . .
7. I'm sure you . . .
8. You're the first to . . .
9. He's trying to . . .
10. She'll send . . .

LESSON 17
Forming Possessives and Plurals

Phonics Class—*workbook, pages 38 and 39*

Review the rule of adding apostrophe and *s* to make a word show ownership. Point out that we are using the same punctuation mark used in contractions.

Review the distinction between possessives and plurals.

ANSWER KEY

Page 38
1.
2. turtle's shell
3. dog's tooth
4. robin's egg
5. cardinal's feather
6. cow's horn
7. butterfly's wings
8. locust's shell
9. Eric's collection

Page 39 (top)

1. s	9. 's
2. 's	10. 's
3. 's	11. 's
4. s	12. s
5. s	13. 's
6. s	14. s
7. 's	15. s
8. 's	16. s

Page 39 (bottom)
1. apostrophe
2. apostrophe

EXTRA ACTIVITY

Let the children search Lesson 17 in the reader for all the different punctuation marks they can find. The story includes commas, question marks, periods, quotation marks, and an apostrophe.

LESSON 18
Review of Endings With *s*

Phonics Class—*workbook, pages 40 and 41*

Review the rule for adding *es* to form plurals.

ANSWER KEY

1. s	6. s
2. s	7. es
3. es	8. es
4. s	9. s
5. es	10. es

Page 40 (bottom) *Each word should have 's on the end followed by an appropriate noun.*

Page 41 *Answers are interchangeable within columns.*

contractions	possessive phrases
didn't	girl's doll
I'll	teacher's plan
we're	Anna's books
can't	Don's shoes
won't	Edna's cat
he'd	dog's tail
they've	Betsy's coat

EXTRA ACTIVITY

Challenge the children to write original sentences each containing a contraction and a possessive.

LESSON 19
Review

Phonics Class—*workbook, pages 42 and 43*

Review any of the lesson material you think needful.

ANSWER KEY

Page 42 (top)

1. qui / et
2. no / tice
3. re / store
4. chuck / le
5. mar / ket
6. pa / per
7. see / saw
8. un / like / ly
9. cab / bage
10. sud / den / ness
11. ker / nel
12. po / em
13. riv / er
14. pud / dle
15. rain / bow
16. de / light / ful
17. li / on
18. cab / in

Page 42 (bottom)

1. ə ô
2. ō ə
3. ŭ ə
4. ə ă
5. ĕ ə
6. ä ə
7. ė ə
8. ə o͞o
9. ė ə
10. ä ə
11. ə ī
12. ā ə

Page 43

1. g
2. a
3. l
4. d
5. h
6. i
7. c
8. j
9. b
10. k
11. e
12. f

Gradebook: 12 points for page 43

LESSON 20
Homophones: ate—eight

Phonics Class—*workbook, pages 44 and 45*

Discuss the term *homophones* (formerly called *homonyms*). Let the children find some pairs on the page and tell the meanings of each word in the pair.

ANSWER   KEY

Page 44

1. b	7. c
2. d	8. b
3. a	9. a
4. c	10. e
5. f	11. f
6. e	12. d

13. f	19. c
14. c	20. e
15. d	21. b
16. a	22. f
17. e	23. a
18. b	24. d

Page 45 (top)

1. eight
2. ate
3. Eight
4. ate
5. ate
6. eight
7. ate
8. eight

Page 45 (bottom)
Individual sentences.

EXTRA   ACTIVITY

Have the children list a word that illustrates an example for each of the items defined on page 43.

LESSON 21
Homophones: week—weak, blew—blue

Phonics Class—*workbook, pages 46 and 47*

Give definitions for the homophones on page 45 and have the children spell the correct words.

ANSWER   KEY

Page 46 (top)

1. weak	5. week
2. week	6. weak
3. week	7. week
4. weak	8. weak

Page 46 (bottom)
Individual sentences.

Page 47 (top)

1. blue	5. blue
2. blew	6. blew
3. blew	7. blue
4. blew	8. blue

Page 47 (bottom)
Individual sentences.

LESSON 22
Homophones: hole—whole, write—right

Phonics Class—*workbook, pages 48 and 49*

Review previous homophones by giving words for the children to spell by definition.

Discuss the two different words spelled *right* and be sure the children realize that either of those meanings get the same spelling in the sentences.

ANSWER KEY

Page 48 (top)

1. hole   5. hole
2. whole   6. whole
3. whole   7. hole
4. whole   8. hole

Page 49 (top)

1. write   5. write, right
2. right   6. right
3. write   7. write
4. right   8. right

Page 48 (bottom)
Individual sentences.

Page 49 (bottom)
Individual sentences.

EXTRA ACTIVITY

Have the children draw lines to separate the syllables in words of more than one syllable in the sentences.

LESSON 23
Homophones: wood—would, hear—here

Phonics Class—*workbook, pages 50 and 51*

Review homophones of previous lessons, spelling by definition.

ANSWER KEY

Page 50 (top)

1. wood   5. would
2. wood   6. wood
3. would   7. would, wood
4. would   8. wood

Page 51 (top)

1. hear   5. hear
2. here   6. hear
3. here   7. hear
4. here   8. here

Page 50 (bottom)
Individual sentences.

Page 51 (bottom)
Individual sentences.

EXTRA ACTIVITY

Have the children make pictures for some of the sentences in the lesson.

LESSON 24
Review

Phonics Class—*workbook, pages 52 and 53*
Review any needed material.

ANSWER KEY

Page 52		Page 53
1. c	9. won—one	1. eight
2. st	10. ¯	2. right
3. dis	11. ˘	3. week
4. est	12. or	4. would
5. oy	13. thank	5. hole
6. ə	14. '	6. hear
7. '	15. can't	7. blue
8. ai		

Gradebook: 22 points for the whole lesson

EXTRA ACTIVITY
Have the children use the name of each person in the class in a possessive phrase.

LESSON 25
Homophones: no—know, their—there

Phonics Class—*workbook, pages 54 and 55*
Explain the second usage of *there* on page 55. Rather than giving a definition, the sentence illustrates the use of *there* to introduce a thought when the verb precedes the subject.

ANSWER KEY

Page 54 (top)		Page 55 (top)	
1. know	5. no	1. There	5. their
2. no	6. no	2. their	6. there
3. know	7. know	3. there	7. their
4. know	8. no	4. there	8. their

Page 54 (bottom)
Individual sentences.

Page 55 (bottom)
Individual sentences.

EXTRA ACTIVITY
Have the children list the books of the Bible on paper.

LESSON 26
Homophones: rode—road, plane—plain

Phonics Class—*workbook, pages 56 and 57*
Review homophones of previous lessons, spelling by definition.

ANSWER KEY

Page 56 (top)

1. road
2. rode
3. road
4. rode, road

5. road
6. rode
7. rode
8. road

Page 57 (top)

1. plain
2. plain
3. plane
4. plane

5. plain
6. plain
7. plain
8. plane

Page 56 (bottom)
Individual sentences.

Page 57 (bottom)
Individual sentences.

EXTRA ACTIVITY

Have the children write 1, 2, or 3 after the sentences in which they printed *plain*, to identify the definition used in each sentence.

LESSON 27
Homophones: deer—dear, see—sea

Phonics Class—*workbook, pages 58 and 59*
Review homophones of previous lessons, spelling by definition.

ANSWER KEY

Page 58 (top)

1. deer
2. dear
3. deer
4. dear, deer
5. dear
6. dear
7. deer
8. deer

Page 58 (bottom)
Individual sentences.

Page 59 (top)

1. see
2. sea
3. see
4. sea
5. see
6. sea
7. see, sea
8. sea

Page 59 (bottom)
Individual sentences.

Gradebook: 26 points for the whole lesson, counting 2 points for each sentence

EXTRA ACTIVITY

Let the children make a picture for some of the sentences.

LESSON 28
Homophones: pair—pear, red—read

Phonics Class—*workbook, pages 60 and 61*
Review homophones of previous lessons, spelling by definition.

ANSWER KEY

Page 60 (top)

1. pear	5. pair, pear
2. pear / pair	6. pair
3. pear	7. pair
4. pear	8. pair

Page 60 (bottom)
Individual sentences.

Page 61 (top)

1. read	5. red
2. Red	6. red
3. red	7. read
4. Red	8. read

Page 61 (bottom)
Individual sentences.

LESSON 29
Homophones: meat—meet, to—too—two

Phonics Class—*workbook, pages 62 and 63*
Review homophones of previous lessons, spelling by definition.

ANSWER KEY

Page 62 (top)

1. meet	5. meet
2. meat	6. meet
3. meat	7. meet
4. meat	8. meat

Page 62 (bottom)
Individual sentences.

Page 63

1. to	7. to
2. too	8. too
3. too	9. two
4. to	10. too
5. two	11. two
6. Two	12. to

EXTRA ACTIVITY
Have the children find the word *to* each time it appears in the sentences on page 63 besides the times they wrote it. Tell them to print the word *to* and the word that follows it each time. They may recognize that each of them is a verb. *To* is the spelling for this usage but it does not mean "in the direction of."

LESSON 30
Review

Phonics Class—*workbook, pages 64 and 65*
Review any material needed.

ANSWER KEY

Page 64

1. plain
2. read
3. know
4. meet
5. road
6. their
7. to
8. sea
9. dear
10. pair

Page 65 (top)

1. d	6. c
2. c	7. d
3. e	8. b
4. b	9. e
5. a	10. a

Page 65 (middle)

1. wouldn't	4. we're
2. she's	5. I've
3. I'm	6. isn't

Page 65 (bottom)

1. si / lent	7. buck / le
2. pad / dle	8. jack / et
3. re / fill	9. grum / ble
4. let / ter	10. spi / der
5. with / out	11. proph / et
6. sci / ence	12. nev / er

13. thun / der / cloud
14. some / what
15. sec / cond
16. fol / low / ing
17. cre / ate
18. won / der / ful

Gradebook: 44 points for the whole lesson

TEST

ANSWER KEY

A.

1. ate	7. know
2. right	8. here
3. week	9. blue
4. wood	10. too / two
5. there	11. see
6. hole	12. plain

B.

1. he is	7. would not
2. I am	8. we have
3. you are	9. is not
4. did not	10. she will
5. can not	11. they are
6. I have	12. will not

C. 1. f   6. f
     2. zh   7. sh
     3. f   8. zh
     4. zh   9. sh
     5. sh   10. sh

D. 1. one, before
     2. after

ra / ven	ped /al
trav / el	no / tice
sev / en	ti / ger
mo / tor	hab / it

3. divide, digraph

nick / el	ei / ther
Ra / chel	rath / er

4. vowels, between

di / et	po / et
flu / id	No / ah

Gradebook: 57 test points

Unit 5

UNIT 5
General Plan

Unit 5 reviews the phonetic structure of our language by presenting the familiar phonograms (called word parts) in a new way. Each letter or combination is presented with all the sounds it makes. Then words are examined part by part and spelled by writing the correct phonogram for the sound of each part.

Directions usually ask for printing in exercises working with word fragments. If you have studied cursive writing, have the children use cursive writing when the directions say "Write" and print when they say "Print."

Pronunciations in this unit are often exaggerated to make the words sound as they are spelled. These shades of pronunciation are readily dropped in the rhythm of normal speech.

Some basic phonics rules are also applied for spelling with silent *e*, soft consonant sounds, and adding suffixes.

Phonics Lessons   Unit 5

Lesson   **Page**

LESSON 1
One-Letter Phonograms Having One Sound

Phonics Class—*workbook, pages 68 and 69*

Introduce Unit 5 as a review of the phonics the children already know. Review the principle that each sound of a spoken word matches a part of the written word. Sometimes more than one letter goes together to represent a sound in the spoken word. The word parts in this lesson are one-letter phonograms which always represent the same sound when considered singly in a pronunciation. (The letter *h* is considered part of a two-letter phonogram in *she*, and so on.)

Encourage children to follow the directions in making as many words as they can. That does not necessarily mean they will have all the blanks filled, but they should not give up quickly.

ANSWER KEY

Page 68

1. *-ar*	3. *-in*	5. *-at*	7. *-ot*
bar	bin	bat	hot
far	fin	fat	dot
jar	din	hat	not
mar	kin	mat	lot
tar	pin	pat	pot
war	tin	tat	tot
	win	rat	rot
		vat	

2. *-eg**	4. *-est*	6. *-ip*	8. *-eep*
beg	best	hip	beep
keg	jest	dip	deep
leg	nest	nip	jeep
peg	lest	lip	keep
	pest	tip	peep
	test	rip	weep
	rest	zip	
	vest		
	west		
	zest		

* Do not expect these blanks to be filled.

Page 69

1. *ca-*	4. *he-*	7. *fi-*	10. *go-*
cab	hem	fib	gob
can	hen	fin	god
cap	hell	fill	got
cat	her	fit	
car		fizz	

2. *mu-*	5. *ta-*	8. *bu-*	11. *si-*
muff	tab	buff	sib
mud	tan	bud	sin
mull	tall	bum	sill
	tap	bun	sip
	tat	bull	sit
	tax	but	six
		buzz	

3. *po-*	6. *bi-*	9. *stu-*	12. *sla-*
pod	bib	stub	slab
pop	bid	stuff	slam
pot	bill	stud	slap
	bin	stun	slat
	bit		

LESSON 2
One-Letter Phonograms Having Two Sounds

Phonics Class—*workbook, pages 70 and 71*

The phonograms in this lesson are spelled with one letter but they do not always have the same sound. Rules are given to tell when *g* and *c* have the soft sounds. You may also discuss the guide that *e* and *i* say the long sound when they are the only vowel and appear at the end of the word or syllable. The letter *s* never says /z/ at the beginning of a word, but there is no rule to determine the sound in all uses.

Page 71 reviews various items concerning the letters of the alphabet. If you think the children do not have these principles mastered, go over the page orally as a class exercise.

ANSWER KEY

Page 70

1. /s/	8. /k/	15. /s/
2. /g/	9. /ĕ/	16. /s/
3. /ĭ/	10. /z/	17. /ē/
4. /j/	11. /g/	18. /s/
5. /ĕ/	12. /ē/	19. /ĭ/
6. /s/	13. /ĭ/	20. /j/
7. /z/	14. /k/	21. /ĭ/

2. a, e, i, o, u
3. y, w
4. f, l, s, z
5. e
6. e, i, y
7. u
8. b i r
   p c j
   u o t

Page 71

1. a b c d e f g h i
   j k l m n o p q r
   s t u v w x y z

LESSON 3
One-Letter Phonograms Having Three Sounds

Phonics Class—*workbook, pages 72 and 73*

Again the rule may be applied that the vowel says its long sound when it is the only vowel and appears at the end of the word or syllable. (The letter *y* as in *baby* is sometimes presented as the short *i* sound.)

The letter *a* says the /ä/ sound when following the /w/ sound, whether it be spelled with *w* or *qu*.

The consonant sound of *y* is /y/.

The third sounds for *o* and *u* are rather incidental and "unruly." The letter *u* may also have a fourth sound, /o͞o/ as in *rude.*

ANSWER KEY

Page 72

1. /ī/	11. /y/	21. /ŏ/	
2. /ă/	12. /ōō/	22. /ōō/	
3. /ŏ/	13. /ō/	23. /ä/	
4. /ū/	14. /ōō/	24. /ū/	
5. /ā/	15. /ā/	25. /ō/	
6. /ē/	16. /ū/	26. /ē/	
7. /ōō/	17. /ī/	27. /ū/	
8. /ōō/	18. /ū/	28. /ā/	
9. /ā/	19. /ā/	29. /ō/	
10. /ä/	20. /y/	30. /ī/	

Page 73

1. scratch	4. offer	7. such	
lap	crops	mud	
2. navy	5. total	8. humid	
David	motor	human	
3. squash	6. to	9. full	
swat	do	pull	

LESSON 4
Two-Letter Consonant Phonograms

Phonics Class—*workbook, pages 74 and 75*

The letters *gh* for the /g/ sound at the beginning of a word have not been presented before. The letters *gh* also say /g/ at the beginning of a syllable as in *aghast* and *afghan*.

The phonogram *qu* is not a digraph. The combination has two sounds and *u* is a consonant in this usage.

ANSWER KEY

Page 74

1. kn	9. gh
2. ng	10. sh
3. wh	11. gn
4. gn sh	12. gh
5. ph	13. wr
6. wh	14. ng
7. mb	15. ck
8. ck	16. gn

17. wh	25. wr ng
18. ck	26. ph
19. sh	27. gn
20. gh	28. qu
21. kn ck	29. ph
22. wh	30. mb
23. ng ng	31. kn
24. qu ck	32. sh

Page 75 (top) *Answers may vary.*

sh ale / *wh* ale   sma *sh* / sma *ck*
bri *ng* / bri *ck*   ri *ng* / ri *ck*
tru *ck*   *sh* ip / *wh* ip
sh adow   *wh* isper

lo *ng* / lo *ck*
wi *sh* / wi *ng* / wi *ck*
tra *sh* / tra *ck*
cra *sh* / cra *ck*

Page 75 (bottom)

1. sign	9. ghost
2. phrase	10. knock
3. wrong	11. track
4. white	12. quack
5. gnash	13. knob
6. knee	14. wreath
7. sing	15. crackle
8. lamb	16. telephone

Two consonants together that make one sound are a consonant *digraph*.

EXTRA ACTIVITY
Have the children list words from page 74 that describe sounds.

LESSON 5
Two-Letter Vowel Phonograms

Phonics Class—*workbook, pages 76 and 77*
Review the vowel-digraph spellings to be used at the end of words. Give some oral spelling practice with the words on page 77.

ANSWER KEY

Page 76 (bottom)
digraph
oy, oi

Page 77

1. t *ai* l	16. sl *ee* p	30. h *oe*
2. d *ay*	17. b *ee*	31. w *oe*
3. aw *ay*	18. fr *ui* t	32. b *oa* t
4. *ai* m	19. s *ee* k	33. s *oa* p
5. pl *ay*	20. j *ui* ce	34. r *oa* st
6. b *ai* l	21. ind *ee* d	35. f *oe*
7. p *ai* nt	22. w *ee* kend	36. d *oe*
8. pr *ay*		
9. str *ay*	23. s *aw*	37. n *oi* se
10. g *ay*	24. l *aw*	38. b *oy*
11. gr *ai* n	25. S *au* l	39. c *oi* l
12. displ *ay*	26. c *au* se	40. destr *oy*
13. tod *ay*	27. r *aw*	41. j *oi* nt
14. afr *ai* d	28. f *au* lt	42. enj *oy*
15. m *ai* n	29. c *au* tion	43. empl *oy*

Gradebook: 46 points for the whole lesson

LESSON 6
More Two-Letter Phonograms

Phonics Class—*workbook, pages 78 and 79*

Have the children pick out and practice saying words with *ti* and *ci*. The correct spelling for the answers on page 79 may be found on page 78.

ANSWER KEY

Page 78

1. ur	11. ur
2. ar ti	12. or
3. ar	13. ur
4. er	14. ti
5. or ti	15. ci
6. ir	16. er
7. ar	17. ar
8. ci	18. ci
9. ir	19. or er
10. er	20. ar er

21. ir	31. or er
22. er	32. ur
23. er	33. ir
24. ur	34. ci
25. ar	35. er or
26. ti	36. ar
27. ur	37. ir
28. ir	38. er
29. ci	39. ti
30. ur	40. ir

Page 79

1. perfect
2. garden
3. border
4. turnip
5. delicious
6. thirsty
7. mention
8. harvest
9. portion
10. partners

EXTRA ACTIVITY

Have the children underline in the word lists on page 78 other two-letter parts they have studied.

LESSON 7
Review

Phonics Class—*workbook, pages 80 and 81*

Practice matching phonograms to spoken sounds. Print a word on the board; then have the children print the letters which spell each of the vocalized sounds as you dictate them one sound at a time. Blends are considered separately because you hear the sound of both letters. After all the parts are printed, the spelling must be identical to the word written as a whole.

The following words may be used for practice.

shack	(Pronounce the parts /sh/, /ă/, /k/.)
toys	(Pronounce /t/, /oi/, /z/.)
wren	(Pronounce /r/, /ĕ/, /n/.)
comb	(Pronounce /k/, /ō/, /m/.)
quail	(Pronounce /kw/, /ā/, /l/.)
seesaw	(Pronounce /s/, /ē/, /s/, /ô/.)
partial	(Pronounce /p/, /är/, /sh/, /ă/, /l/.)
noisy	(Pronounce /n/, /oi/, /z/, /ē/.)
caution	(Pronounce /k/, /ô/, /sh/, /ŏ/, /n/.)
elephant	(Pronounce /ĕ/, /l/, /ĕ/, /f/, /ă/, /n/, /t/.)

Make it clear that the separation of individual sounds does not indicate syllables.

ANSWER KEY

Pages 80 and 81 *Each word will have individual sentences.*

1. t o d ay
2. d e s t r oy
3. kn ee
4. c l ai m
5. w i s d o m
6. h ar v e s t
7. gn aw
8. qu a ck
9. d ai s y

LESSON 8
Two-Letter Vowel Phonograms Having Two Sounds

Phonics Class—*workbook, pages 82 and 83*

Practice some oral spelling of the words on page 82.

ANSWER KEY

Page 82

1. oo	/o͞o/	11. ew	/ū/	21. oo	/o͝o/
2. ow	/ō/	12. oo	/o͞o/	22. ow	/ō/
3. ue	/o͞o/	13. ew	/o͞o/	23. ow	/ou/
4. ew	/o͞o/	14. ue	/o͞o/	24. ew	/o͞o/
5. oo	/o͞o/	15. oo	/o͞o/	25. ow	/ō/
6. ow	/ō/	16. ow	/ou/	26. oo	/o͞o/
7. oo	/o͞o/	17. ue	/ū/	27. oo	/o͞o/
8. ew	/ū/	18. ow	/ou/	28. ew	/ū/
9. ue	/o͞o/	19. oo	/o͞o/	29. oo	/o͝o/
10. oo	/o͞o/	20. ow	/ō/	30. ew	/o͞o/

Page 83

1. book	6. drew	11. mew
2. crown	7. slow	12. raccoon
3. few	8. cool	13. soon
4. snow	9. true	14. allow
5. spool	10. wood	15. blue / hue

LESSON 9
Two-Letter Vowel Phonograms Having Two Sounds

Phonics Class—*workbook, pages 84 and 85*

Have the children read the word lists orally to be sure they can read the words. Discuss word meanings for any unfamiliar words.

Some of the words are homophones. The spellings given on page 84 are expected for the answers on page 85.

ANSWER KEY

Page 84

1. ey	/ā/	11. ei	/ā/
2. ey	/ē/	12. ei	/ē/
3. ey	/ē/	13. ei	/ā/
4. ey	/ē/	14. ei	/ē/
5. ey	/ā/	15. ei	/ē/
6. ey	/ā/	16. ei	/ā/
7. ey	/ā/	17. ei	/ā/
8. ey	/ē/	18. ei	/ē/
9. ey	/ā/	19. ei	/ē/
10. ey	/ē/	20. ei	/ē/
		21. ie	/ē/
		22. ie	/ē/
		23. ie	/ī/
		24. ie	/ē/
		25. ie	/ī/
		26. ie	/ī/
		27. ie	/ī/
		28. ie	/ē/
		29. ie	/ē/
		30. ie	/ē/

Page 85

1. lie	16. deceive
2. pied	17. piece
3. die	18. seize
4. tie	19. monkey
5. they	20. journey
6. prey	21. niece
7. reign / rein	22. receive
8. rein / reign	23. brief
9. obey	24. chief
10. vein	25. ceiling
11. hey	26. valley
12. veil	27. believe
13. disobey	28. either
14. key	29. priest
15. neither	30. chimney

EXTRA ACTIVITY

Have the children write all the homophones they can identify for words in the list on page 84.

pray	rain	dye
hay	seas	lye
vale	vain	peace

LESSON 10
Two-letter Phonograms Having Two Sounds

Phonics Class—*workbook, pages 86 and 87*

Practice reading the words orally.

Do a few crossword puzzle samples with the children to teach them how to use the sounds given to narrow down possibilities for answers.

You may want to wait to do the puzzle until page 86 is checked. Then the children may use the sounds they have printed as a reliable guide.

ANSWER KEY

Page 86

1. th	/th/		11. th	/th/
2. ch	/ch/		12. ch	/ch/
3. si	/sh/		13. si	/sh/
4. th	/th/		14. ch	/k/
5. th	/th/		15. si	/sh/
6. ch	/k/		16. th	/th/
7. ch	/ch/		17. ch	/ch/
8. th	/th/		18. si	/zh/
9. si	/zh/		19. th	/th/
10. Ch	/k/		20. th	/th/

21. si	/zh/
22. ch	/ch/
23. th	/th/
24. th	/th/
25. ch	/k/
26. ch	/ch/
27. th	/th/
28. si	/sh/
29. ch	/ch/
30. th	/th/

Page 87

Across	Down
4. thumb	1. discussion
7. decision	2. schedule
8. chrome	3. mission
9. Christian	4. thorns
12. school	5. much
13. division	6. those
14. chain	10. there
	11. moth

Gradebook: 45 points for the whole lesson

EXTRA ACTIVITY

Have the children print the number of syllables for each word on page 86, following the sound they printed.

LESSON 11
Two-Letter Phonograms Having Three Sounds

Phonics Class—*workbook, pages 88 and 89*

Let the children find samples of the different sounds for each spelling in the list on page 88.

ANSWER KEY

Page 88

1. ed	/ĕd/	11. ed	/t/	21. ea	/ā/
2. ou	/ōō/	12. ed	/d/	22. ou	/ou/
3. ea	/ē/	13. ea	/ē/	23. ea	/ĕ/
4. ed	/t/	14. ed	/d/	24. ea	/ē/
5. ed	/t/	15. ou	/ōō/	25. ou	/ou/
6. ea	/ā/	16. ea	/ĕ/	26. ea	/ē/
7. ed	/t/	17. ou	/ou/	27. ea	/ĕ/
8. ou	/ōō/	18. ed	/ĕd/	28. ed	/ĕd/
9. ea	/ā/	19. ou	/ŭ/	29. ed	/d/
10. ou	/ŭ/	20. ed	/d/	30. ea	/ĕ/

Page 89

1. h **ou** se
2. tr **ou** ble
3. h **ea** d
4. gr **ou** p
5. gr **ea** t
6. want **ed**
7. watch **ed**

LESSON 12
Review of Phonograms

Phonics Class—*workbook, pages 90 and 91*

Do some class practice with words on the board, matching word parts you have studied to spoken sounds. Use current reading vocabulary words to encourage the concept that this principle works largely for all words beyond selected phonics lists. You will meet snags here and there in exceptional words, but most words can be reasonably explained with these phonograms.

ANSWER KEY

Pages 90 and 91 *Each word will
have individual sentences.*

1. o b ey
2. v ei n
3. kn ew
4. g r ou p
5. f ea s t ed
6. f r ui t
7. th or n y
8. c o n f u si o n
9. d e l i ci ou s

LESSON 13
More Review of Phonograms

Phonics Class—*workbook, pages 92 and 93*

Practice some more words with the class.

ANSWER KEY

Pages 92 and 93

1. sh ie l d
2. y aw n
3. g r a ph
4. t o mb
5. t ur k ey
6. f ew
7. wr u ng
8. j ui c y
9. gh o s t
10. s c ou t

11. wh y
12. l oa n ed
13. s m oo th
14. w i sh ed
15. b r ea k i ng
16. s ch oo l
17. j au n t
18. sh ow
19. th r ea d
20. c ei l i ng

LESSON 14
Three-Letter Phonograms

Phonics Class—*workbook, pages 94 and 95*

The combination *wor* is actually two phonograms, but may be taught as one three-letter phonogram to distinguish this *or* from the one that says /ôr/.

Have the children practice reading the word lists.

ANSWER KEY

Page 94 (middle)

1. ear
2. igh
3. wor
4. wor
5. dge
6. ear
7. igh

8. wor
9. ear
10. wor
11. igh
12. ear
13. dge
14. dge

15. igh
16. wor
17. ear
18. dge
19. igh
20. dge
21. wor

22. dge
23. igh
24. igh
25. ear
26. wor
27. ear
28. igh

Page 94 (bottom)

1. We f *ir* st h *ear* d the
   v *er* se in ch *ur* ch
   w *or* ship.

2. Are the cl *er* k's *ear* nings
   w *or* th a th *ir* d p *ur* se?

3. The *ear* ly n *ur* se w *or* ked
   on h *er* sk *ir* t.

4. Do little b *ir* d s l *ear* n to
   p *er* ch in t *ur* n for
   w *or* ms?

Page 95

1. girl
   firm
   shirt
   skirt
   thirsty
   birthday
2. church
   hurt
   burp
   turn
   murmur
   burden

3. her
   fern
   stern
   clerk
4. work
   worm
   worst
   worth
5. earth
   search
   pearl
   yearn

Gradebook: 72 points for the whole lesson

EXTRA ACTIVITY

Have the children write all the words they can find in Lesson 14 in the reader containing the digraph *ea* and print the sound of *ea* after each word.

LESSON 15
Four-Letter Phonograms

Phonics Class—*workbook, pages 96 and 97*

Study the examples in class and let the children try some oral spelling of these words.

Have the word list on page 97 read orally and discuss the meaning of any words the children do not know.

ANSWER KEY

Page 96

1. through
2. bough
3. caught
4. tough
5. weigh
6. daughter
7. laugh
8. trough
9. dough
10. laughing
11. bought
12. eight
13. though
14. fought

Page 97

1. dough
2. daughter
3. weighty
4. bough
5. ought
6. tough
7. trough
8. through
9. taught
10. thought
11. neigh
12. laughter

LESSON 16
Identifying Sounds in Words

Phonics Class—*workbook, pages 98 and 99*

This lesson illustrates the fact that a single phonogram may have various sounds. Print any of the phonograms on the board and ask the class to give all of the sounds that it can make.

Begin the lesson as a class activity.

ANSWER KEY

Page 98

1. /ĕ/	13. /ä/	25. /ō/
2. /ē/	14. /y/	26. /ou/
3. /ĭ/	15. /ē/	27. /ōō/
4. /ī/	16. /ĭ/	28. /ū/
5. /s/	17. /ŏ/	29. /ōō/
6. /z/	18. /ō/	30. /ē/
7. /g/	19. /ōō/	31. /ā/
8. /j/	20. /ōō/	32. /ē/
9. /k/	21. /ū/	33. /ā/
10. /s/	22. /ŭ/	34. /ē/
11. /ā/	23. /ōō/	35. /ē/
12. /ă/	24. /ōō/	36. /ī/

Page 99

37. /ch/	52. /j/	67. /m/
38. /k/	53. /ĭ/	68. /n/
39. /th/	54. /ėr/	69. /n/
40. /th	55. /ėr/	70. /r/
41. /sh/	56. /ā/	71. /g/
42. /zh/	57. /ăf/	72. /f/
43. /ĕ/	58. /ô/	73. /ē/
44. /ā/	59. /ou/	74. /ā/
45. /ē/	60. /ôf/	75. /ā/
46. /ĕd/	61. /ō/	76. /ô/
47. /t/	62. /ŭf/	77. /ô/
48. /d/	63. /ô/	78. /ō/
49. /ō/	64. /ōō/	79. /oi/
50. /ŭ/	65. /sh/	80. /ō/
51. /ōō/	66. /sh/	81. /ėr/

LESSON 17
Identifying More Sounds in Words

Phonics Class—*workbook, pages 100 and 101*

This lesson illustrates the fact that various phonograms can produce the same sound. Voice a sound and ask the children to print on the board as many different spellings as they can for that sound.

ANSWER KEY

Page 100

1. /f/	13. /d/	25. /ū/
2. /f/	14. /d/	26. /ū/
3. /m/	15. /t/	27. /n/
4. /m/	16. /t/	28. /n/
5. /r/	17. /ĕ/	29. /n/
6. /r/	18. /ĕ/	30. /ou/
7. /g/	19. /ŭ/	31. /ou/
8. /g/	20. /ŭ/	32. /ou/
9. /s/	21. /ōō/	33. /k/
10. /s/	22. /ōō/	34. /k/
11. /z/	23. /oi/	35. /k/
12. /z/	24. /oi/	36. /k/

Page 101

37. /sh/	52. /ī/	67. /ē/
38. /sh/	53. /ī/	68. /ē/
39. /sh/	54. /ī/	69. /ē/
40. /sh/	55. /ėr/	70. /ē/
41. /ô/	56. /ėr/	71. /ē/
42. /ô/	57. /ėr/	72. /ē/
43. /ô/	58. /ėr/	73. /ā/
44. /ô/	59. /ėr/	74. /ā/
45. /ô/	60. /ōō/	75. /ā/
46. /ō/	61. /ōō/	76. /ā/
47. /ō/	62. /ōō/	77. /ā/
48. /ō/	63. /ōō/	78. /ā/
49. /ō/	64. /ōō/	79. /ā/
50. /ō/	65. /ōō/	80. /j/
51. /ī/	66. /ē/	81. /j/

EXTRA ACTIVITY

Let an older student pro- nounce words from the lesson for the children to spell orally, or let the children give words to each other to spell.

LESSON 18
Review of Phonograms

Phonics Class—*workbook, pages 102 and 103*
Self-explanatory.

ANSWER KEY

Pages 102 and 103 *Each word will have individual sentences.*
1. h ear d
2. b ir th d ay
3. s qu ir m
4. m er c y
5. h igh e s t
6. th ough t f u l
7. l augh
8. th ough
9. w eigh

Gradebook: 27 points for the lesson, allowing 2 points for each sentence—1 for correct usage and 1 for form (capitalization and punctuation)

LESSON 19
Spelling

Phonics Class—*workbook, pages 104 and 105*

Which spelling shall we use for a spoken sound when there is more than one way to spell that sound? Rules help us in some of the choices. Review the vowel digraphs and diphthongs not used at the end of a word. Review the letters that indicate the soft sound of *c* or *g*, and the spelling of /ẻr/ after *w*. Review the rule for using *c* or *k* before certain vowels.

Some of the time we need to depend on familiarity with the word to know which spelling to use. Do not expect the children to do perfect spelling by sound, but after printing the sounds, have them compare the words given at the end of the lesson and correct any errors.

ANSWER KEY

Pages 104 and 105
1. z oo   zoo
2. f ai l   fail
3. p ea ch   peach
4. s i x   six
5. c oi n   coin
6. w or d   word

7. s l ow	slow
8. h ea d	head
9. b r i dge	bridge
10. p o ck e t	pocket
11. f a th er	father
12. b r igh t	bright
13. ear l y	early
14. a r ou n d	around
15. n a ti o n	nation

EXTRA ACTIVITY

Can the children handle a dictionary? Let them practice looking up the words in this lesson. It may be interesting to copy the pronunciation given in the dictionary onto the phonics page beside the pronunciation given there. That will reveal differences of symbols and shades of pronunciation.

LESSON 20
Silent Final *e*—Rule 1

Phonics Class—*workbook, pages 106 and 107*

Review the principle that silent *e* gives a vowel in the word the long sound. Let the children do some oral spelling of long vowel words.

ANSWER KEY

Page 106

1. note	13. cape
2. tube	14. tote
3. tape	15. cube
4. hope	16. bite
5. ripe	17. hate
6. robe	18. dune
7. dime	19. nape
8. cute	20. made
9. use	21. slate
10. kite	22. bathe
11. tone	23. paste
12. hide	24. clothe

Page 107

1. kite, kit
2. not, note
3. dim, dime
4. cap, cape
5. us, use
6. tube, tub
7. tape, tap
8. cut, cute
9. hide, hid
10. bit, bite
11. paste, past

LESSON 21
Silent Final *e*—Rule 2

Phonics Class—*workbook, pages 108 and 109*
Sometimes there is a silent *e* on the end of a word that has a short vowel. Or the word has a vowel digraph and does not need the *e* to give it the long vowel sound. It may be there to let a *c* or *g* have the soft sound.
Let the children practice some oral spelling of these words.

ANSWER KEY

Page 108 (top)

1. ce	5. ge	9. ce	13. ce
2. ce	6. ce	10. ge	14. ce
3. ce	7. ge	11. ge	15. ge
4. ge	8. ge	12. ce	16. ce

Page 108 (bottom) *Each blank should have an* e *printed in it.*

Page 109
Rule 1

grape	mule	stone
throne	lime	slide
strike	trade	cube

Rule 2

hinge	edge	prance
force	forge	ledge
merge	once	since

Rules 1 and 2

age	page	race
rice	mice	huge
face	nice	cage

EXTRA ACTIVITY
Let someone pronounce words from the lesson for the children to spell orally.

LESSON 22
Silent Final *e*—Rule 3

Phonics Class—*workbook, pages 110 and 111*
Teach the rule of adding *e* to any word that ends with the /v/ sound. Have the children practice it in oral spelling.

ANSWER KEY

Page 110 (top) *Each blank should have an* e *printed in it.*

Page 110 (middle)

1. carve	4. have	7. peeve
2. deserve	5. live	8. serve
3. give	6. nerve	9. weave

Page 110 (bottom)

1. dive	6. hive
2. save	7. cove
3. cave	8. rave
4. five	9. wove
5. wave	10. pave

Page 111 (top)

Rule 1—silent, end, vowel, long

Rule 2—*e*, end, *c*, *g*, soft

Rule 3—end, *v*

Gradebook: 69 points for the whole lesson

Page 111 (bottom)

1. 2	11. 3	21. 1
2. 1	12. 2	22. 3
3. 2	13. 3	23. 2
4. 3	14. 3	24. 1
5. 2	15. 1	25. 3
6. 3	16. 2	26. 2
7. 2	17. 3	27. 3
8. 1	18. 1	28. 1
9. 2	19. 2	29. 3
10. 1	20. 1	30. 1

LESSON 23
Silent Final *e*—Rule 4

Phonics Class—*workbook, pages 112 and 113*

Discuss the rule that every syllable must contain a vowel. A silent final e provides a vowel for these syllables. Review the syllabication of such words and remind the children not to divide *ck*.

ANSWER KEY

Page 112

1. nee / dle   dle
2. muf / fle   fle
3. ta / ble   ble
4. stee / ple   ple
5. ket / tle   tle
6. bu / gle   gle
7. puz / zle   zle
8. an / kle   kle
9. i / dle   dle
10. un / cle   cle
11. driz / zle   zle
12. waf / fle   fle
13. mar / ble   ble
14. bum / ble   ble
15. sim / ple   ple
16. fiz / zle   zle
17. cack / le   le
18. lit / tle   tle
19. ea / gle   gle
20. pud / dle   dle
21. tram / ple   ple
22. wig / gle   gle
23. han / dle   dle
24. daz / zle   zle
25. snif / fle   fle
26. star / tle   tle
27. bot / tle   tle
28. ap / ple   ple
29. tan / gle   gle
30. speck / le   le
31. wrin / kle   kle
32. shuf / fle   fle
33. buck / le   le
34. tick / le   le
35. snug / gle   gle
36. bub / ble   ble

Page 113 *Individual sentences and pictures are expected.*

EXTRA ACTIVITY

Alphabetize each of the first two columns of words on page 112.

LESSON 24
Silent Final *e* in Other Words

Phonics Class—*workbook, pages 114 and 115*
Read the word lists and practice some oral spelling.

ANSWER KEY

Page 114 (top) *Each blank should have an* e *printed on it.*

Page 114 (bottom) and 115
1. promise, engine
2. mouse, noise
3. verse, were, are, horse
4. cause
5. freeze, loose, raise,
   cheese, breathe, ease,
   please, goose
6. cheese, breathe, there
7. a. goose
   b. mouse
   c. horse
   d. cheese
   e. engine
   f. noise
   g. verse

LESSON 25
Review of Final *e* Rules

Phonics Class—*workbook, pages 116 and 117*
   You may want to conduct some oral spelling practice with the words in the lesson, or have the children spell some of them on the board and discuss the correct letters for the sounds.
   Word that may merit attention are listed below with some explanation.

puzzle, puddle, giggle, battle—The last syllable has three letters. The first syllable needs to end with a consonant because it has a short vowel sound. So these words have double consonants.

single—The letter *g* appears as part of the /ng/ sound in the pronunciation and again in the second syllable. But the word has two consonants in the middle and does not need two *g*'s.

fence, choice, voice, chance—In these words, the /s/ sound is the soft *c*.

plunge, fudge, edge, fringe—In these words, the /j/ sound is the soft *g*. The phonogram *dge* follows a short vowel when there is no consonant sound between.

came, carve—Remember /k/ is spelled with *c* before *a*, *o*, or *u*.

ANSWER KEY

Page 116 (top)

Rule 1—e, end, word, vowel, word
Rule 2—silent, word, soft
Rule 3—words, *v*
Rule 4—syllable, vowel

Pages 116 (bottom) and 117

1. are	5	6. came	1
2. give	3	7. choice	2
3. house	5	8. serve	3
4. puzzle	4	9. puddle	4
5. fence	2	10. noise	5

Page 117

11. pride	1	26. noble	4
12. plunge	2	27. tube	1
13. staple	4	28. starve	3
14. love	3	29. voice	2
15. cause	5	30. some	5
16. hope	1	31. worse	5
17. nerve	3	32. have	3
18. fume	1	33. live	3
19. fudge	2	34. vote	1
20. edge	2	35. giggle	4
21. where	5	36. fringe	2
22. grade	1	37. chance	2
23. carve	3	38. battle	4
24. single	4	39. chime	1
25. mumble	4	40. tense	5

LESSON 26
Drop Final *e* to Add Suffixes

Phonics Class—*workbook, pages 118 and 119*
Review the rule presented in this lesson.

ANSWER KEY

Page 118

1. smiled	smiling
2. pasted	pasting
3. pleased	pleasing
4. decided	deciding
5. received	receiving
6. behaved	behaving
7. tamer	tamest
8. finer	finest
9. surer	surest
10. coarser	coarsest
11. larger	largest
12. fiercer	fiercest

Page 119

13. famous	20. admirable
14. nervous	21. storage
15. desirous	22. mileage
16. liken	23. spinal
17. hasten	24. natural
18. worsen	25. service
19. notable	26. typist

EXTRA ACTIVITY

Have the children find which final *e* rule fits each of the root words given in the lesson.

LESSON 27
Double Consonant to Add Suffixes

Phonics Class—*workbook, pages 120 and 121*
Review the rule for doubling consonants to add suffixes. Apply the rule to the last syllable of a word if the accent falls on the last syllable. The modified vowel in number 2 on page 120 and the /ėr/ sound on page 121 are considered as having the short sound.

ANSWER KEY

Page 120

1. drummer yes yes yes yes
2. stormy yes yes no yes
3. baggage yes yes yes yes
4. drainage yes no yes yes
5. thicken yes yes no yes
6. gladness yes yes yes no

7. forbidden
8. cancerous
9. dependable
10. unloading
11. preferred
12. carpeting
13. admittance
14. occurrence

Page 121
1. forgetting
2. forgetful
3. forgotten
4. dangerous
5. referred
6. beginner

Gradebook: 44 points for the whole lesson

EXTRA ACTIVITY
Ask the children to write sentences with some of the words they wrote on page 121.

LESSON 28
Spelling Rules for *ei* and *ie*

Phonics Class—*workbook, pages 122 and 123*
Go over the directions on page 122 with the class and have the children spell some words orally for each section.
Discuss the rule in the directions on page 123 and do some of the answers in class. Caution the children to work carefully so they do not confuse their *e*'s and *i*'s.

ANSWER KEY

Page 122 (top)
1. v *ei* l
2. r *ei* n
3. v *ei* n
4. sk *ei* n

Page 122 (middle)
5. sl *eigh*
6. *eigh* t
7. fr *eigh* t
8. n *eigh*
9. w *eigh*
10. w *eigh* t
11. n *eigh* bor
12. *eigh* teen

Page 122 (bottom)

1. p *ie*	9. d *ie* s
2. t *ie*	10. t *ie* d
3. d *ie*	11. pr *ie* d
4. l *ie*	12. sk *ie* s
5. fr *ie* s	13. tr *ie* d
6. tr *ie* s	14. den *ie* d
7. p *ie* s	15. appl *ie* d
8. l *ie* s	16. p *ie* d

EXTRA ACTIVITY

Have someone spell the letters of words from the lesson and see if the children can say the words that are spelled without seeing them.

Page 123

1. br *ie* f	16. dec *ei* ve
2. rec *ei* ve	17. rel *ie* f
3. n *ie* ce	18. misch *ie* f
4. c *ei* ling	19. perc *ei* ve
5. pr *ie* st	20. gr *ie* f
6. f *ie* ld	21. bel *ie* ve
7. ch *ie* f	22. dec *ei* t
8. p *ie* ce	23. br *ie* fly
9. rec *ei* ver	24. ach *ie* ve
10. conc *ei* t	25. conc *ei* ted
11. rel *ie* ve	26. bel *ie* f
12. dec *ei* tful	27. s *ie* ge
13. conc *ei* ve	28. perc *ei* ved
14. pon *ie* s	29. f *ie* rce
15. bab *ie* s	30. rec *ei* pt

LESSON 29
Spelling With *ei* and *ie*

Phonics Class—*workbook, pages 124 and 125*

Review the rules for *ie* and *ei* spellings as given in Lesson 28. Some of the words in this lesson have homophones with other spellings. You may want to do the first three words with the class as a caution against using the homophones.

Syllables beginning with /s/ are spelled with soft *c*.

Review rule 3 for silent final *e*.

ANSWER KEY

Pages 124 and 125

1. v ei l	veil	7. ch ie f	chief
2. v ei n	vein	8. d e c ei ve	deceive
3. w eigh	weigh	9. p r ie s t	priest
4. n eigh b or	neighbor	10. c ei l i ng	ceiling
5. t ie	tie	11. r e c ei ve	receive
6. t r ie d	tried	12. b e l ie ve	believe

LESSON 30
Spelling Homophones

Phonics Class—*workbook, pages 126 and 127*

If the children need help, do the lesson orally, writing the homophones on the board and discussing their meanings. Then have the children write sentences independently.

Progressive students may be able to do the lesson on their own.

ANSWER KEY

Pages 126 and 127 *One word from each pair will have individual sentences.*

1. sea, see
2. right, write
3. blew, blue
4. know, no
5. road, rode
6. mail, male
7. weak, week
8. heard, herd
9. way, weigh
10. threw, through

TEST

ANSWER KEY

A.

1. mb	16. eigh	31. aw
2. kn	17. ei	32. u
3. wr	18. ea	33. ough
4. ph	19. y	34. ou
5. dge	20. ey	35. o
6. g	21. ie	36. ew
7. c	22. y	37. er
8. ti	23. ie	38. ear
9. ci	24. igh	39. ur
10. si	25. ow	40. or
11. ai	26. ough	41. ir
12. ay	27. oe	42. ough
13. ey	28. ou	43. augh
14. ei	29. augh	44. ough
15. ea	30. au	45. s / si

B. 1.
```
f        ch
k        ph
n ————— kn
r        mb
m        wr
```
2.
```
ti        ur
er        ai
ay        oy
oi        ou
ow        ci
```

3.
```
eigh      ue
igh       au
oa        ey
ew        ie
aw        ough
```

4.
```
ea ——————ie
z         dge
oo        ui
g         s
ch ————— k
```

C.

Rule 1	Rule 2
cute	charge
made	fence
write	mince
bone	hinge

Rule 3	Rule 4
have	bubble
give	handle
carve	eagle
serve	turtle

No rule

horse	were
some	cause

Gradebook: 85 test points

PHONICS RULES USED IN GRADE TWO

The numbers at the right tell where the rule is introduced. The first number indicates the unit and the second number is the lesson.

A. Sound and Spelling Rules

1. The /k/ sound   1:5
   a. Use *c* before *a*, *o*, or *u*.
   b. Use *k* before *e* or *i*.
   c. Use *ck* after short vowel sounds.
2. Final silent *e*
   a. A silent final *e* lets another vowel in the word say its long sound.   1:6
   b. A silent final *e* lets a *c* or *g* before it have the soft sound.   5:21
   c. Do not end words with *v*. Add a silent *e*.   5:22
   d. Every syllable must have a vowel. Silent *e* is added to words like *apple*, *table*, *marble*, etc.   5:23
3. Spellings for the end of words
   a. Use *ay* for the /ā/ sound at the end of a word.   1:11
   b. Use *oy* for the /oi/ sound at the end of a word.   2:2
   c. Use *ow* for the /ou/ sound at the end of a word, and when the word ends with *l* or *n*.   2:2
4. Double *f*, *l*, *s*, or *z* at the end of a short vowel word.   1:17
5. The vowels *y* and *w*
   a. The letter *y* is a vowel when it says /ī/, /ē/, or is part of a digraph or diphthong.   2:11
   b. The letter *w* is a vowel when it is a part of a digraph or diphthong.   2:11
6. The letters *or* say /ėr/ when they follow *w*.   2:3
7. Soft consonant sounds
   a. The letter *c* says /s/ when it comes before *e*, *i*, or *y*.   2:13
   b. The letter *g* says /j/ when it comes before *e*, *i*, or *y*.   2:14
8. When a vowel follows *bu* or *gu*, the u is silent.   2:16
9. In spelling *ei* or *ie* use *ie* unless it follows *c* or the vowel sound is /ā/.   5:28

B. Symbols

1. The macron (ˉ) marks long vowel sounds.   1:6
2. The apostrophe (')
   a. The apostrophe may represent an indistinct vowel sound.   2:26
   b. The apostrophe is used with *s* to show possession.   2:24
   c. The apostrophe indicates missing letters in a contraction.   4:14
3. The accent mark (') shows which syllable is stressed in pronunciation.   3:18

4. The schwa (ə) represents an indistinct vowel sound in an
   unaccented syllable.   3:21
5. The breve (˘) marks short vowel sounds.   3:24

C. Definitions of Terms
1. A **digraph** is two letters together that make one sound. 1:19
2. A **blend** is two letters that make two sounds close together. 1:21
3. A **diphthong** is two vowel sounds in one syllable.   2:2
4. A **modified vowel** is changed by *r*.   2:3
5. **Controlled a** says /ô/ (usually followed by *w*, *u*, or *l*). 2:6
6. **Suffixes** are letters added at the end of words.   2:7
7. **Prefixes** are letters added at the beginning of words.   3:9
8. A **compound word** is made from two words put together.   2:29
9. **Homophones** are different words that sound alike.   4:20

D. Adding Suffixes
1. Add *es* instead of *s* when a word ends with *x*, *s*, *sh*, or *ch*. 2:7
2. When a one-syllable word with a short vowel ends with one
   consonant, double the consonant before adding a suffix that
   begins with a vowel.   3:1
3. Rule 2 applies to the second syllable of two-syllable words if
   the accent falls on the second syllable.   5:27
4. When a word ends with a silent *e*, drop the *e* before adding a
   suffix that begins with a vowel.   3:3
5. When a word ends with *y* after a consonant, we usually change
   the *y* to *i* before adding a suffix (unless the suffix begins with *i*). 3:6,7

E. Dividing Syllables
1. Divide words between prefixes, root words, and suffixes.   3:11
2. Divide words between two consonants.   3:12, 13
3. Divide compound words between the smaller words.   3:13
4. Words that end with *le*
   a. Most words that end with *le* are divided with three letters
      in the second syllable.   3:15
   b. Do not divide *ck*. The letters *le* alone form the second syllable
      when they follow *ck*.   3:16
5. Words with one consonant in the middle
   a. Divide before the consonant if the first syllable has a long
      vowel.   4:7
   b. Divide after the consonant if the first syllable has a short
      vowel.   4:8
6. Divide a word between the vowels when two vowels come
   together and both vowels sound.   4:12